Sex, God, and Marriage

Sex, God, and Marriage

Johann Christoph Arnold

THE PLOUGH PUBLISHING HOUSE

Published by The Plough Publishing House
of The Bruderhof Foundation, Inc., Farmington, PA 15437 USA
and by Bruderhof Communities in the UK
Robertsbridge, East Sussex TN32 5DR UK.

ISBN: 0-87486-923-4

09 08 07 06 05 04 03 02 10 9 8 7 6 5 4 3 2 1

Original Title: *A Plea for Purity*
First Edition, 1996: ISBN 0-87486-072-5
Second Edition, 1998: ISBN 0-87486-960-9

A catalog record for this book is available
from the British Library.

Printed in USA

Preface

Five years ago we published the first edition of *Sex, God, and Marriage.* Since then readers have responded to it as to no other Plough title. It seems the book has touched a tender nerve. Some find its message out of sync with "reality." Others say it unsettles them more than they would like to admit. The vast majority have written to say how grateful they are for the clear yet compassionate guidance it offers.

If the past is any indication, *Sex, God, and Marriage* will continue to prompt many more responses and spark new discussion. Granted, it is a book whose message few in our present age care to hear. But for those who listen, it holds a promise. A reader recently wrote to us to say, "All my past relationships failed because they were built on sex, not God. *Sex, God, and Marriage* has given me insight into how a true relationship and marriage should be." May it do the same for many more.

The Editors
April 2002

To my faithful wife, Verena,
without whose help
this book would not have been possible.

Other Titles by the Author

Be Not Afraid: Overcoming the Fear of Death

Escape Routes: For People Who Feel Trapped in Life's Hells

Endangered: Your Child in a Hostile World

Seeking Peace: Notes and Conversations along the Way

Cries from the Heart: Stories of Struggle and Hope

Drained: Stories of People Who Wanted More

Why Forgive?

Contents

The author with Pope John Paul II, New York City, October 1995

"I was glad to deliver *Sex, God, and Marriage* to the Holy Father. He was very happy for this ecumenical gesture and, more than that, for the contents and for the harmony of moral conviction that springs from our common faith in Christ. Such conviction will inevitably arouse hatred, even persecution. The Lord has predicted it. But with him we must continue in trying to overcome evil through good."

From a letter, Joseph Cardinal Ratzinger
to Johann Christoph Arnold, December 1995

Foreword

In *Sex, God, and Marriage* we find a message needed today in every part of the world. To be pure, to remain pure, can only come at a price, the price of knowing God and of loving him enough to do his will. He will always give us the strength we need to keep purity as something beautiful for God. Purity is the fruit of prayer. If families pray together they will remain in unity and purity, and love each other as God loves each one of them. A pure heart is the carrier of God's love, and where there is love, there is unity, joy, and peace.

M. Teresa MC

Mother Teresa of Calcutta
November 1995

Introduction

Everywhere today, people are searching for lasting and meaningful relationships. The myth of romance continues to be taken for granted by millions, and a new generation of young men and women has accepted the belief that sexual freedom is the key to fulfillment. But as desperately as people want to believe in the sexual revolution of the last few decades, it is clear to many of them that something has gone terribly wrong. Instead of bringing freedom, the sexual revolution has left countless wounded and isolated souls. As we face the great anguish around us, it is more important than ever for all of us, young and old, to consider the direction of our lives and ask ourselves where we are headed.

The twenty-first century heralds the loss of the clear teachings of the Old and New Testaments on marriage and the relationship of the sexes. We have turned against God and rebelled against his order of creation, and we have justified our rebellion with human arguments. We have ignored the words of Jesus and scorned the voice of the Spirit. But we have found neither freedom nor fulfillment.

As a pastor I have counseled many people over the years, both single and married. For many of them, the sexual sphere is not an area of joy but one of frustration, confusion, and even despair. People look for unity of heart and soul with one another, but they are so blinded by the notion of romantic love that their deepest longings remain obscured. They know that marriage and sexual union is a gift from God; that it should be the most intimate and rewarding relationship a man and a woman can share. But they wonder why it has become the source of such loneliness and pain for them and for so many others.

I am no social scientist. But if the findings of recent studies have made anything clear it is this: the fallout caused by our culture's acceptance of casual sex is socially devastating. More than half of all marriages in the United States fail. Almost forty percent of America's children live in different houses than their biological fathers. Poverty, violent crime, delinquency, promiscuity, alcohol and drug abuse, mental illness, and suicide are all rooted in the breakdown of the family and the erosion of the marriage bond.

At the same time, those who save sexual activity until marriage (though their numbers are dwindling) are far less likely to have an affair or divorce, and those who commit themselves to one lifelong partner lead happier lives.[1]

While current trends point to continuing decay, there are encouraging signs that people are beginning to call into question the thrills of cheap sex and the seeming ease of uncommitted love. This is especially true among "GenXers." There is an increased yearning among young people to find genuine relationships and to build secure homes, giving renewed hope that a two-parent family is still possible.

Again and again I have seen that when people are willing to surrender their lives to Jesus, they are able to find a way out of their unhappiness. Once people have the courage and humility to face his call to repentance, he can bring them lasting freedom and happiness.

Jesus brings true revolution. He is the original source of love, because he is Love itself. His teaching is neither a matter of prudishness nor of permissiveness: he offers his followers an entirely different way. He brings a purity that liberates us from sin and leads to the possibility of a completely new life.

There is very little in today's culture that nurtures or protects the new life that Jesus wants to give us. People talk incessantly about the importance of committed marriages and wholesome family life, but how many of us are willing to take action to make these values a concrete reality? Many of us are tempted to blame society for the influences that corrupt us. But what about us so-called Christians? How many of us are ready to unplug the television set and take a hard look at our own marriages and relationships and our personal lives? How many of us actually support the brothers and sisters around us in the daily struggle for purity? How many of us stick out our necks to confront the sin in each other's lives? How many of us are really accountable?

There is tremendous pain among those who claim to be followers of Christ: broken families, battered wives, neglected and abused children, and sinful relationships. Yet instead of an outcry, there is indifference. When will we wake up and realize that our apathy is destroying us?

More than ever, we need to come back to an understanding of the church as a living body of committed members who share life in practical deeds of love. But we must start with ourselves first and then see where we can encourage those around us. We need to know our youth well enough to be able to guide them as they seek relationships and lifetime commitments; we need to provide ongoing support for the marriages around us; we need to work for healing when our brothers or sisters stumble or fall – and accept their help when we ourselves have fallen.

Most of all, we must show the world that the unique teachings of Jesus and his apostles are the only answer to the spirit of our time. That is why I have put together this little book. I am neither a biblical scholar nor a professional therapist, and I am fully aware that most of what I have written is completely contrary to popular wisdom. But I do feel the urgent need to share my certainty that Jesus' call to a life of love, purity, honesty, and commitment is our only hope.

This is not only a personal book – it comes out of the life of the church community I serve, and everything in it reflects the concerns and experiences of its members. My hope is that all of us – all men and women of our time – might stop to reconsider God's purpose for sex and marriage.

Sadly, too many people today have simply given up on the possibility of a pure life. They have bought into the myth of sexual "liberation" and tried to live with its disappointments, and when their relationships fall apart, they explain away their failures. They fail to see what a tremendous gift purity is.

All the same, I believe that deep in every heart there is a yearning for unclouded relationships and for a love that lasts. It takes courage and self-discipline to really *live* a different way, but it is possible. Wherever there is a faithful church – a community of people who are committed to living in genuine and honest relationships – there is help and hope for every person and every marriage. May this book give each reader that faith.

J.C.A.

In the Beginning

CHAPTER I

In the Image of God

God said, "Let us make man in our image and likeness to rule the fish in the sea, the birds of heaven, the cattle, all wild animals on earth, and all reptiles that crawl upon the earth." So God created man in his own image; in the image of God he created him, male and female. God blessed them and said to them, "Be fruitful and increase; fill the earth and subdue it."

Genesis 1:26–28

In the opening chapter of the story of creation we read that God created humankind – both male and female – in his own image, and that he blessed them and commanded them to be fruitful and to care for the earth. Right from the start, God shows himself as the creator who "saw all that he had made, and it was very good." Here, right at the beginning of the Bible, God reveals his heart to us. Here we discover God's plan for our lives.

Many, if not most, twentieth-century Christians dismiss the story of creation as a myth. Others insist that only the strictest, most literal interpretation of Genesis is valid. I simply have reverence for the word of the Bible as it stands. On the one hand, I would not think of arguing away anything in it; on the other, I believe scientists are right in cautioning that the biblical account of creation should not be taken too literally. As Peter says, "With the Lord, a day is like a thousand years, and a thousand years like one day" (2 Pet. 3:8).

God's image sets us apart.

Exactly how human beings were created remains a mystery for the creator alone to unveil. Yet I am sure of one thing: no person can find meaning or purpose without God. Rather than dismiss the creation story simply because we do not understand it, we need to find its inner, true meaning and rediscover its significance for us today.

In our depraved age, reverence for God's plan as described in Genesis has been almost completely lost. We do not treasure the meaning of creation enough – the significance of both man and woman as creatures formed in the image and likeness of God. This likeness sets us apart in a special way from the rest of creation and makes each human life sacred (Gen. 9:6). To view life in any other way – for instance, to view others only in the light of their usefulness, and not as God sees them – is to disregard their worth and dignity.

What does creation "in God's image" mean? It means that we are to be a living picture of who God is. It means that we are to be co-workers who further his work of creating and nurturing life. It means that we belong to him, and that our being, our very existence, should always remain related to him and bound to his authority. The moment we separate ourselves from God we lose sight of our purpose here on earth.

In Genesis we read that we have the living spirit of God: "The Lord God formed man from the dust of the ground and breathed into his nostrils the breath of life, and man became a living being" (Gen. 2:7). In giving us his spirit, God made us responsible beings who possess the freedom to think and act, and to do so in love.

But even if we possess a living spirit, we remain only images of the creator. And when we look at creation in a God-centered, not human-centered, way we will understand our true place in his divine order of things. The person who denies that God is his origin, who denies that God is a living reality in his life, will soon be lost in a terrible emptiness. Ultimately, he will find himself trapped in the self-idolatry that brings with it self-contempt and a contempt for the worth of others.

All of us long for what is imperishable.

What would we be if God had not breathed his breath into us? Darwin's whole theory of evolution, by itself, is dangerous and futile because it is not God-centered. Something inside each of us cries out against the idea that we have been hatched by a purposeless universe. Deep within the human spirit is a thirst for what is lasting and imperishable.

Since we are made in God's image, and God is eternal, we cannot, at the end of life, merely vanish again like smoke. Our life is rooted in eternity. Christoph Blumhardt* writes, "Our lives bear the mark of eternity, of the eternal God who created us to be his image. He does not want us to be swallowed up in the transitory, but calls us to himself, to what is eternal."[2]

God has set eternity in our hearts, and deep within each of us is a longing for eternity. When we deny this and live

* Christoph Friedrich Blumhardt (1842–1919), German pastor, author, and religious socialist.

only for the present, everything that happens to us in life will remain cloaked in tormenting riddles, and we will remain deeply dissatisfied. This is especially true in the sexual area. Casual sex desecrates the soul's yearning and capacity for that which is eternal. No person, no human arrangement, can ever fill the longing of our souls.

The voice of eternity speaks most directly to our conscience. Therefore the conscience is perhaps the deepest element within us. It warns, rouses, and commands us in our God-given task (Rom. 2:14–16). And every time the soul is wounded, our conscience makes us painfully aware of it. If we listen to our conscience, it can guide us. When we are separated from God, however, our conscience will waver and go astray. This is true not only for an individual, but also for a marriage.

Already in Genesis, chapter 2, we read about the importance of marriage. When God created Adam, he said that everything he had made was good. Then he created woman to be a helpmate and partner to man, because he saw that it was not good for man to be alone. This is a deep mystery: man and woman – the masculine and the feminine – belong together as a picture of who God is, and both can be found in him. Together they become what neither would be apart and alone.

Everything created by God gives us an insight into his nature – mighty mountains, immense oceans, rivers, and great expanses of water; storms, thunder and lightning, huge icebergs; meadows, flowers, trees, and ferns. There is power, harshness, and manliness, but there is also gentleness, motherliness, and sensitivity. And just as the various forms of life in nature do not exist without each other, God's children, too, male and female, do not exist alone.

They are different, but they are both made in God's image, and they need each other to fulfill their true destinies.

When God's image is defaced, life's relationships lose purpose.

It is a tragedy that in much of today's society the differences between man and woman are blurred and distorted. The pure, natural image of God is being destroyed. There is endless talk about women's equality, but in practice women are abused and exploited more than ever before. In films, on television, in magazines, and on billboards the ideal woman (and increasingly, the ideal man) is portrayed as a mere sex object.

Generally speaking, marriages in our society are no longer regarded as sacred. Increasingly they are seen as experiments or as contracts between two people who measure everything in terms of their own interests. When marriages fail, there is almost always the option of no-fault divorce, and after that a new attempt at marriage with a new partner. Many people no longer even bother to make promises of faithfulness; they just live together. Women who bear and raise children or stay married to the same husband are sometimes scorned. And even when their marriage is a healthy one, they are often seen as victims of oppression who need to be "rescued" from male domination.

Children are often no longer treasured. In Genesis, God commanded, "Be fruitful and increase." Today we avoid the "burden" of unwanted offspring by means of legalized abortion. Children are viewed as a bother; they are too expensive to be brought into the world, to be raised, to be given a college education. They are an economic strain on our materialistic lives. They are even too time-consuming to love.

Is it any wonder that so many in our time have lost hope? That so many have given up on the possibility of enduring love? Life has lost its value; it has become cheap; most people no longer see it as a gift from God. Advances in biomedical engineering and in fetus screening techniques enable growing numbers of couples to choose an abortion for selfish reasons. Without God, life is absurd, and there is only darkness and the deep wound of separation from him.

Despite the efforts of many dedicated individuals, the church today has failed miserably in grappling with this situation. All the more, each of us must go back to the beginning and ask ourselves once again, "Why did God create man and woman in the first place?" God created every person in his image, and he has set a specific task for every man, woman, and child on this earth, a task he expects us to fulfill. No one can disregard God's purpose for his creation or for himself without suffering deep inner need (Ps. 7:14–16).

The materialism of our time has emptied life of moral and spiritual purpose. It hinders us from seeing the world with awe and wonder, and it hinders us from seeing our true task. The sickness of soul and spirit brought about by consumerism has eaten so deeply into our conscience that it is no longer able to mirror good and evil clearly. Yet there is still a deep-seated need in each of us that makes us long for goodness.

We will find healing only if we believe firmly that God created us and that he is the giver of life, love, and mercy. As we read in the third chapter of the Gospel of John, "God so loved the world that he gave his only son, that whoever believes in him should not perish but have eternal life. For God sent his son into the world, not to condemn the world, but that the world might be saved through him."

In God's son – in Jesus – the creator's image appears with utmost clarity and finality (Col. 1:15). As the perfect image of God, and as the only way to the Father, he brings us life and unity, joy and fulfillment. Only when our life is lived in him can we experience his truth and goodness, and only in him can we find our true destiny. This destiny is to be God's image; to rule over the earth in his spirit, which is the creative, life-giving spirit of love.

CHAPTER 2

It Is Not Good for Man to Be Alone

Then the Lord God said, "It is not good for the man to be alone. I will provide a partner for him..." So the Lord God caused the man to fall into a deep sleep; and while he was sleeping, he took one of the man's ribs and closed up the place with flesh. Then the Lord God made a woman from the rib he had taken out of the man, and he brought her to the man. Then the man said, "Now this at last is bone of my bones and flesh of my flesh; she shall be called 'woman,' for she was taken out of man."

Genesis 2:18, 21–23

There is little that is so difficult for a person to bear as loneliness. Prisoners held in solitary confinement have told of rejoicing to see even a spider – at least it is *something* alive. God created us to be communal beings. Yet our modern world is frighteningly devoid of relationships. In many areas of life, technological progress has resulted in the deterioration of community. Increasingly, technology has made people seem unnecessary.

As the elderly are placed into retirement communities or personal-care homes, as factory workers are replaced by hi-tech robotics, as young men and women search year after year for meaningful work, they fall into despair and hopelessness. Some depend on the help of therapists or psychologists, and others seek avenues of escape such as alcoholism, drugs, and suicide. Cut off from God and each other, thousands of people lead lives of quiet desperation.

To live in isolation from others kills this unity and leads to despair. Thomas Merton writes:

> Despair is the absolute extreme of self-love. It is reached when a man deliberately turns his back on all help from anyone else in order to taste the rotten luxury of knowing himself to be lost...
>
> Despair is the ultimate development of a pride so great and so stiff-necked that it selects the absolute misery of damnation rather than accept happiness from the hands of God and thereby acknowledge that he is above us and that we are not capable of fulfilling our destiny ourselves.
>
> But a man who is truly humble cannot despair, because in a humble man there is no longer any such thing as self-pity.[3]

We see here that pride is a curse that leads to death. Humility, however, leads to love. Love is the greatest gift given to humankind; it is our true calling. It is the "yes" to life, the "yes" to community. Love alone fulfills the longing of our innermost being.

God created us to live with and for others.

God has planted in each of us an instinctive longing to achieve a closer likeness to him, a longing that urges us toward love, community, and unity. In his last prayer, Jesus points out the importance of this longing: "May they all be one, as thou, Father, art in me, and I in thee, so also may they be in us, that the world may believe that thou didst send me" (John 17:20–21).

No one can truly live without love: it is God's will for every person to be the "thou" for every other. Every person is called to love and help those around him on God's behalf (Gen. 4:8–10).

God wants us to find community with one another and to help one another in love. And there is no doubt that when we meet our brother's or sister's inmost heart, we can help them, for "our" help is given by God himself. As John says, "We know that we have passed out of death into life, because we love our brethren. He who does not love abides in death" (1 John 3:14). Our lives are fulfilled only when love is kindled, proved, and brought to fruition.

Jesus tells us that the two most important commandments are to love God with our whole heart, soul, and strength, and to love our neighbor as ourselves. And these two commandments cannot be separated: love to God must always mean love to one's neighbor. We cannot find a relationship to God if we disregard others (1 John 4:19–21). Our way to God must be through our brothers and sisters, and in marriage, through our partner.

If we are filled with God's love, we can never be lonely or withdrawn for long; we will always find someone to love. God and our neighbor will always be near us. All we need to do is find them. Recently a young man in my community shared with me his newly discovered joy in reaching out to others. Sean had been living in Baltimore doing volunteer work building homes for the disadvantaged. He thought that this would be enough. However, when he came home at the end of the day he didn't know what to do:

> I found myself wasting away in front of the television. My zest for life was rapidly diminishing. Then someone told me about an evening tutoring program for inner-city children. They were desperately looking for help. So I decided to check it out. Now I help out every night. I can't believe how my whole perspective on life has changed. I never knew before how much I needed to love these children.

When we suffer from loneliness, it is often simply because we desire to be loved rather than to give love. Real happiness comes from giving love to others. We need to seek community of love with our neighbor again and again, and in this seeking we must each become a helper, a brother or a sister. Let us ask God to free our choked-up hearts for this love, knowing that we can find it only in the humility of the cross.

Every person can be an instrument of God's love.

In the story of the creation of Adam and Eve it is clear that man and woman were created to help, to support, to complement each other. What a joy it must have been for God to bring woman to man – and man to woman! Because we are all made in the image of God, in his likeness, we must all find each other in joy and love, whether we are married or not.

By bringing Eve to Adam, God shows all humans their true calling – to be helpers who reveal his love to the world. And by bringing us his son, Jesus, he shows us that he will never leave us lonely or without help. Jesus himself said, "I will not leave you orphaned; I will come to you." He promises us that "the one who has received my commandments and obeys them – he it is who loves me; and he who loves me will be loved by my Father; and I will love him and disclose myself to him" (John 14:18–21).

Who can understand the depth of these words and the hope they bring to our troubled world? The loneliest, most discouraged, disillusioned people may be assured that God will never forsake them. Even if they are unable to find human friendship, they will never be alone as long as they hold on to God.

God brought Adam and Eve together to heal their loneliness and to set them free from their one-sidedness, and he has the same plan for every man and woman he brings together in marriage. Yet marriage in itself cannot bring wholeness. Unless we abide in Christ, we will bear no fruit. When we love him who alone is our support, our hope, and our life, we can be secure in knowing and loving one another. But if we isolate ourselves inwardly from Christ, nothing will go well. He alone holds everything together and gives us access to God and to others (Col. 1:17–20).

God is the source and the object of true love.

Marriage is not the highest goal of life. God's image is reflected most brightly and completely where there is love first for him and then for our brothers and sisters. In a true Christian marriage, then, the husband will lead his wife and children not to himself, but to God. In the same way, a wife will support her husband as a helper, and together they will lead their children to honor them as father and mother, and to love God as their creator.

To be a helper to another on God's behalf is not just an obligation, but a gift. How different our relationships would be if we rediscovered this! We live in a time when fear and mistrust grip us everywhere we go. Where is love, the love that builds community and the church?

There are two kinds of love. One is turned selflessly toward others and their well-being. The other is possessive and limited to the ego. Augustine says, "Love is the self of the soul, the hand of the soul. When it holds one thing, it cannot hold something else. If it is to hold what one gives it, it has to put down what it is holding."[4] God's love desires nothing. It gives and sacrifices itself, for this is its joy.

Love always has its roots in God. May God grant that the power of his love grips us anew. It will lead us to others, to share our lives with them. More than that, it will lead us to the kingdom. Love is the secret of God's coming kingdom.

CHAPTER 3

They Shall Become One Flesh

For this reason a man will leave his father and mother and be united to his wife, and they will become one flesh.

Genesis 2:24

Marriage is sacred. In the Old Testament, the prophets use it to describe God's relationship with his people Israel: "I will betroth you to me forever; I will betroth you in righteousness and justice, in love and compassion. I will betroth you in faithfulness, and you will acknowledge the Lord" (Hos. 2:19). God reveals his love to all people in a special way in the unique bond between husband and wife.

Marriage is more than living happily together.

In the New Testament, marriage is used as a symbol for the unity of Christ with his church. In the Gospel of John, Jesus is compared to a bridegroom, and in Revelation we read that "the wedding of the Lamb has come, and his bride has made herself ready" (Rev. 19:7–9).

It is not without significance that Jesus changed water into wine at a wedding; clearly, he had great joy in marriage.

Yet it is equally clear that to Jesus, marriage is a holy matter. He takes it so seriously that he speaks with uncompromising sharpness against even the slightest step toward its destruction: "Therefore what God has joined together, let no one separate" (Matt. 19:6–9).

We can see from Jesus' sharpness what a horror adultery is in the eyes of God. The whole Bible protests against it, from the books of the Prophets, where the idol worship of the children of Israel is called adultery (Jer. 13:25–27), to Revelation, where we read of God's wrath against the harlot. When the bond of marriage is broken, love – the unity of spirit and soul between two – is broken and smashed, and not only between the adulterer and his spouse, but between himself and God.

In our present-day culture, the institution of marriage is teetering on the brink of disaster. Much of what is called love is nothing but selfish desire. Even in marriage many couples live together selfishly. People are deceived in thinking that fulfillment can be found without sacrifice and faithfulness, and even though they may live together, they are afraid to love each other unconditionally.

Still, amid millions of floundering and ruined marriages, God's love stands eternal and cries out for constancy and devotion. There is a voice deep within each of us, however muffled, that calls us back to faithfulness. On some level, all of us yearn to be united – with free and open hearts – to somebody, to some other "thou." And if we turn to God in the trust that such unity with another is possible, we can find the fulfillment of our longing.

True fulfillment comes from giving love to another person. Yet love does not only seek to give; it also longs to unite. If I really love another person, I will be interested in knowing what is in him and willing to be led out of my one-sidedness. In love and humility I will help him to the possibility of a full awakening, first toward God, and then toward others. True love is never possessive. It always leads to the freedom of faithfulness and purity.

The faithfulness between a husband and wife is a reflection of God's eternal faithfulness, for it is God who brings every true bond together. In God's faithfulness we find the strength to let love flow through our lives, and to let our gifts unfold for each other. In the love and unity of the church it is possible to become of one spirit with every brother and sister, and also to become of one heart and soul with them (Acts 4:32).

Sexual love can give God's love visible form.

There is a difference between the love of an engaged or married couple and the love among other men and women. Nowhere is a person more dependent on another than in marriage. There is a special joy in the heart of a married person when the beloved is near; and even when separated, there is a unique bond between them. Through the intimate relationship of marriage, something takes place which may even show in a couple's faces. As von Gagern,* says, "Often it is only through his wife that the husband becomes truly a man; and through her husband that the wife gains true womanhood."[5]

In a true marriage, each partner seeks the fulfillment of the other. By complementing each other, the union between husband and wife is enhanced. In their love for one another, through their faithfulness to one another, and in

* Friedrich E. F. von Gagern (1914–) German Catholic psychiatrist. See "For Further Reading."

their fruitfulness, husband and wife reflect God's image in a mysterious and wonderful way.

In the unique bond of marriage we discover the deeper meaning of becoming one flesh. Obviously to become one flesh means to become one physically and sexually, but it is far more than that! It is a symbol of two people bound and melted together, heart, body, and soul, in mutual giving and total oneness.

When two people become one flesh, they are no longer two, but actually one. Their union is the fruit of more than companionship or partnership; it is the deepest intimacy. As Friedrich Nietzsche writes, it is brought about by "the resolve of two to create a unity which is more than those who created it. It is reverence for one another and for the fulfillment of such a resolve."[6]

Only in this reverence and oneness does marriage fulfill the demands of the sexual conscience. Through the will to have children, to be fruitful and to multiply, and through the togetherness that reflects the unity of God with his creation and his people, marriage gives visible form to God's outpouring love.

When God is at the center of a marriage, full unity of heart, soul, and body is possible.

In God's order of marriage there are at least three different levels of experience. The first, most wonderful level is unity of spirit: the oneness of heart and soul in God. In this oneness we can have community not only with our spouse but with all believing persons. The second level is unity of emotion: the current of love from one heart toward another that is so strong that a person can, so to speak, hear the heartbeat of another. The third level is physical unity: the expression of oneness found when two bodies are fused in perfect union.

Too many couples today are content with the third level alone, or perhaps the second. A marriage based only on the physical and emotional is doomed to disappointment. Even though waves of emotional or physical attraction are natural, they can leave deep wounds if they are not placed under Christ. Not long ago a woman I know told me that she and her husband had only joined my congregation because they wanted to have a church wedding – not because they were interested in committing their lives to God. "My husband and I never talked about God's vision for our lives, or about what we wanted before or after our marriage," she writes. "We were not on the same wavelength." Now her husband has deserted her and their five children. It has become painfully clear to her that because their commitment to each other was not grounded in Christ, she and her husband lacked a solid, lasting foundation for their marriage.

If a marriage is to be truly healthy, it must be founded in the order of God – on unity of spirit, heart, and soul. Most people today, including those of us who claim to be Christians, have no idea how much God has prepared for those who truly love and honor him. When we embrace God's order for our relationships, we will experience God's blessings. The experiences of the heart that God can give in a true engagement or marriage are greater than we can imagine. Too many of us live only in the world of the senses – of sleeping, eating, and drinking – and never take time to really turn to what is much more vital: our inner life. This is also true in so many marriages today. Sex is the focal point, and often unity of heart is not even sought or mentioned. Is it any wonder that so few couples remain faithful to each other for life?

Anyone who has lived near the ocean knows something of nature's power in the pull of high and low tides. In marriage, as in friendship, there are high and low tides. When a relationship is at low ebb, it is all too easy for us to lose patience, to distance ourselves from our partner, and even to abandon efforts toward a renewal of love. When God is at the center, we can turn to him and find faith and strength even at our lowest ebb.

The more we live up to the image of God in which we are created, the more strongly will we sense that God must remain our center, and that his commandments are fitting for us. We will sense that his commandments are not laid on us as alien laws and commands. Rather, we will see that they are in keeping with our true nature as created in his image. But the more we betray and destroy God's image within us, the more his rulership will appear to us as something foreign, a moral compulsion that crushes us.

To be fruitful for each other, by complementing each other in love, and to be fruitful with each other in bearing children – it is these purposes that make marriage blessed and holy, and a joy in heaven. Even so, in the story of the creation, before God's command "to be fruitful," comes a blessing: his gift of a partner to the first man. In giving the man this gift, it is as if God is saying, "My image lives in you." Whenever we approach marriage, we must consider this with great reverence. In every person and in every marriage lives the potential for a genuine expression of the image of God.[7]

CHAPTER 4

The First Sin

Now the serpent was more crafty than any of the wild animals the Lord God had made. He said to the woman, "Did God really forbid you to eat from any tree in the garden?" "You will not surely die," the serpent said to the woman. "For God knows that when you eat of it your eyes will be opened, and you will be like God, knowing good and evil."

Genesis 3:1, 4–5

When God created the world, he saw that every thing he made was good. The earth was truly his kingdom, and life was ruled by the spirit of peace. Everything, including man and woman, dwelled together in unity and harmony and took delight in one another and in all that God had made. With trembling reverence and wonder Adam and Eve stood before the life-filled tree in the Garden of Eden. But then the serpent misled Adam and Eve. Immediately, evil came into God's creation and tried to destroy it completely.

Eve was tempted by the serpent with one simple question: "Did God really say that?" and with one simple promise: "Surely you will not die!" It is important that we understand what this means. Satan, the seducer, tempted Eve with words of God, just as later he tempted Jesus with words of God.

Pride separates us from God and from each other.

What else was it, if not pride, when Eve looked at the tree and lusted for its fruit, wanting to make herself like God? Was she not testing God to see whether he would really keep his word? The serpent put doubt into her heart, and Eve listened to him with great curiosity. That in itself was a betrayal of God, and it gives us an insight into how Satan still works today.

Satan still wants to separate us from God, from our brothers and sisters, and from our neighbor. And if we are not watchful, he can do it simply by asking a seemingly innocent question that sows seeds of mistrust and division in our hearts. Satan disguises himself as an angel of light (2 Cor. 11:14), but actually he is the slanderer, the twister of truth, the father of lies, the murderer from the beginning; he tries to throw us into disorder and confusion and doubt – and very often he succeeds.

In the Gospel of Matthew we read that shortly after Jesus' baptism, when he withdrew into the wilderness, Satan tried to tempt him. Knowing that Jesus was physically weak after fasting for forty days, Satan approached Jesus with a face of compassion and showed false reverence by suggesting that all the kingdoms of the world should belong to him.

Yet already in that first temptation, Jesus recognized Satan as the tempter, and the twister of truth. He trusted in God unconditionally and did not consider listening to

Satan for even a moment, but rather went the way of trust, obedience, and dependence on God. Satan could not come close to his heart.

It was not just the forbidden fruit that enticed Adam and Eve, but pride and the self-seeking desire to be like God. Because they lacked trust, obedience, and dependence, they cut themselves off from God. In the end, because they no longer honored him, they made idols of each other.

The greatest curse on our human destiny is the attempt to become like God. Bonhoeffer says, "In following Satan's temptations to be like God yet independent of him, man has become a god against God."[8] The result is a deep sickness in the human spirit. The image of God is now a stolen image, and twisted by idolatry and rebellion against him, it brings great darkness and need (Rom. 1:23–32).

False love hinders the joy of total giving.

Adam and Eve both sinned against love. They were deceived by a false love. How many things happen today that go by the name of love and are nothing but destruction and soul-murder!

> True love wants the person of God to shine through the beloved: God remains the value by which love is measured and the final goal of love's striving. But man, in a false love to the beloved, turns away from the highest good and thereby makes it impossible for God to shine through the beloved.[9]

All this should be a serious warning to us, whether we are married or hoping to be married. God alone must be first in our lives, not our partner, not our children. In our own marriage, my wife and I learned that when God did not have the first and foremost place in our relationship, and when we did not turn to him for guidance even in small matters, we soon lost our closeness to each other. This affected our children too (even if they were not conscious of it), by making them disobedient and quarrelsome. I have seen the same occur in many families: when a couple drifts apart, their children act out their insecurities. In our case, as with many other couples, once my wife and I turned back to God and sought to rebuild our relationship, our children responded.

When we idolize our partner or our children, our love becomes false. We cannot speak freely about our shortcomings or those of our family. Like Adam, we no longer truly love God or see his countenance; we see only our spouse's or our children's. Rather than address issues head-on, we gloss things over. In this way, we eventually lose touch with God and with each other. Worse, we open the door to evil, especially in the sexual area, and to inner deadness and isolation. Adam and Eve lost their innocence because they lost their unity with God. And through the terrible emptiness that followed, man blamed woman and sought to dominate, and woman, resentful of man, blamed Satan. All unity was destroyed, and man and woman became rivals and were no longer one (Gen. 3:7–19).

When our marriages are separated from God, rivalry soon takes root and selfishness rules us. In competing with our partner to rule the roost, we strive to create our own little paradise on our own terms, and we soon sink into emptiness and deep discontent. Our inner bond is destroyed and we remain bound to one another only through infatuation. We continually blame each other and seek our own advantage and independence. The joy of total giving is gone and only the curse of half-heartedness is left.

The enemy of life in God is an independent and covetous will. As my grandfather Eberhard Arnold* writes, this will is "the commercial spirit of mammon, the legal spirit of property-based relationships, the detachment of sexual desire from the soul and from unity and community of spirit...All this is death; it is no longer connected with life."[10]

Anything that stands in opposition to life and love is evil, and we should never underestimate the power of evil. Sin always leads to separation, and the wages of sin are always death (Rom. 6:23). Sinful pride bears its bitter fruit in estrangement, separation from God, from our true selves, from others, and from the earth. Satan and sin shatter the most fundamental relationships we have.

From ancient times on, Christians have pictured Satan as a creature with hooves and horns. Such a notion has no biblical basis. Satan and his demons surround the earth as a force of evil – like an atmosphere (Eph. 2:1–2; 6:12). His sole aim is to blind humans with self-interest and egoism: "You will be like God." And instead of going the way of simple obedience, we allow ourselves to be tempted.

Like Adam and Eve, all of us are divided and estranged by our sin.

Adam and Eve's first sin symbolizes the fall of each one of us. We cannot ignore the fact that the original image of God in us has been terribly distorted. Instead of being content to reflect the image of God, we strive for equality with God. We have turned the highest qualities within us

* Eberhard Arnold (1883–1935); writer, theologian, and founder of the Bruderhof, an international movement of Christian communities.

against God's will. In our worldly "freedom" we are no longer even concerned about God or his original image. We are estranged from him and moved only by the affairs of the world. We are at odds with ourselves and trapped by the guilt of our own dividedness.

Cut off from God in this way, we place ourselves at the center of the universe and try to find peace in possessions and pleasure. But these idols only leave us troubled with anxiety and anguish. Then arises the first mistrustful question, "Why?" and the second, "Is God really there?" We begin to doubt the guidance of the Spirit, and we ask, "Why do I have it so hard? Why me?"

Such questions eat away at our trust, not only in God but in each other, and when we ask them we are never far from sinning. Complete trust takes the hand that God is offering and goes the way he leads. Even if the way leads through darkness or suffering, through hard places, over rocks and deserts, trust will help us to follow. If we take God's hand, nothing can happen to us. But as soon as we let go of God and question him, we will begin to despair. That is always the challenge: to hold on to God.

Jesus had to endure every human suffering; he was spared nothing – not hunger, thirst, loneliness, nor torment. But he did not attempt to escape from his misery. He is near to us, and he is always ready to help us, to give us the strength to overcome (Heb. 2:14–18). Even the most satanic temptations, the most terrible hours of darkness, are overcome by these words of Jesus: "You shall worship the Lord your God, and him alone shall you serve" (Matt. 4:10). This is the secret. Here Satan loses all power over us, and the first sin no longer binds.

CHAPTER 5

Restoring the Image of God

> The Lord is the Spirit, and where the Spirit of the Lord is, there is freedom. And we, who with unveiled faces all reflect the Lord's glory, are being transformed into his likeness with ever-increasing glory, which comes from the Lord, who is the Spirit...Therefore, if anyone is in Christ, he is a new creation; the old has gone, the new has come!
>
> *2 Corinthians 3:17–18; 5:17*

Stronger than any human relationship is our relationship to God. All other relationships are merely symbols of it. First and foremost, we are images of God and we need to find reverence for that fact again and again.

The greatest hope for every seeker, and for every relationship or marriage, is to recognize that even though we have distorted this image and fallen away from God, a faint reflection still remains in us. Despite our corruption, God does not want us to lose our destiny as creatures made in his image. Therefore he sent his son Jesus, the second Adam, to break into our hearts (Rom. 5:17–19). Through Jesus the image of God can be restored in every man and woman, and to every relationship.

Jesus opens the way to God and to each other.

Jesus is God's reconciler: he has come to reconcile us to God and to others and to overcome the inner discord in our lives (Eph. 2:11–19). When we become discouraged or downcast, then more than ever we must seek him. Everyone who seeks will find God. This is a promise. Jeremiah says, "You will seek me and find me when you seek me with all your heart" (Jer. 29:13). And there are the wonderful words in the gospels: "Anyone who seeks will find; to anyone who knocks, the door will be opened" (Luke 11:10). These words are true today, and if we take them seriously, God will become living in our hearts.

The way to God is open for everyone. No human being is excluded from this gift, because Jesus came as a human being. God sent him to restore his image in us. Through him we have access to the Father. But this can only happen when the experience of Pentecost – the experience of personal repentance, conversion, and faith – becomes a burning reality for us.

The miracle of Pentecost, in which the Spirit descended to earth in power and love, can happen anywhere in the world at any time. It can happen wherever people cry out, "Brothers, sisters, what shall we do?" and wherever they are ready to hear the age-old answer of Peter, "Repent and be baptized, every one of you, in the name of Jesus the Messiah, for the forgiveness of your sins...Save yourselves from this crooked generation" (Acts 2:37–40).

Freedom comes through surrender, not human strength.

We can find forgiveness and salvation only at the cross. At the cross we undergo death. This death liberates us from everything that has prevented fellowship with God and with others and renews our relationship with them. In giving up the sin and evil which has enslaved us, we find freedom in Jesus. We can never redeem ourselves or better ourselves by our own strength. All we can finally do is surrender ourselves completely to Jesus and his love, so that our lives no longer belong to us but to him.

My father, J. Heinrich Arnold, writes:

> If we want to be healed of the wounds made by Satan's tricks and arrows...we must have the same absolute trust in Jesus as he had in God. Ultimately, all we have is our sin. But we must lay our sin before him in trust. Then he will give us forgiveness, cleansing, and peace of heart; and these lead to a love that cannot be described.[11]

What does it mean to "lay our sin before him in trust?" Freedom and the possibility for reconciliation begin whenever we confess the accusations of our conscience. Sin lives in darkness and wants to remain there. But when, as the following story of an acquaintance, Darlene, shows, we bring to light the sins that burden us – when we admit them without reserve – we can be cleansed and freed:

> By the ninth grade, I had picked out my "future husband." I spent many secret hours writing to him in my diary, dreaming about him, and watching his house in the hope of seeing him through a window. Several years later he married someone else, and my fantasy world fell apart.

Through my high school years I tried to be part of the "in" crowd, always conscious of what I said, did, and wore. But by the time I graduated, I had flirted with countless boys, and though I felt guilty about this because of my upbringing, I simply chose to ignore it. I squashed my protesting conscience and convinced myself that I could handle any situation.

After high school I traveled to Israel, intending to spend a year at a kibbutz. At first I was shocked by the constant partying and the preoccupation with sex among the teens there, but soon I was hanging out in guys' rooms and going to drinking parties and discos like everyone else. I told myself I could withdraw from any situation at any time, but within weeks I had let myself be sucked into relationship with a boy who said he truly loved me. I wanted so much to believe him that I fell for him, even though I knew he was the Don Juan of the kibbutz. I felt more and more guilty; I could see I was doing exactly what I had claimed I was strong enough to resist. I panicked when I saw him a few nights later with another girl.

I returned home and, during the next two years, thought I had overcome my problem. But I had not. I fell again.

A man promised me a wonderful future, and he told me constantly how much he loved me and how beautiful I was. I wanted desperately to believe in him. Soon it was handholding, hugging, kissing, touching – one thing led to the next. As he wanted more and more from me, I completely blocked out all feelings of terrible guilt and horror. When he asked for sex, I gave in. I chose to fall deeper into sin rather than face up to the absolute mess I was in. I wanted to run away from home and live with him, and I promised him my love and loyalty – even when he threatened to kill me if I told anyone about our relationship. The next day he disappeared, and I never saw him again.

Plagued by depression, I considered suicide. My head and stomach ached incessantly. I felt I was going insane. I was

> obsessed with sex; I didn't see how I could go on without a man to "love" me. I went for one boy after another; two of them were even engaged to other girls. I grew desperate and wept secretly for hours. Through it all, though I felt like a prostitute, I tried to show my family and friends a happy and confident image...
>
> My double life could not last forever, and eventually I was caught in a lie. I realized then that God was giving me another chance. I might never again have such an opportunity to break out of my sin. Giving in, I turned to my parents and confessed everything. The devil was not quick to let me go, tormenting me in my sleep, but the depth of God's love became very real to me in the following weeks and months. There were constant prayers and love from my family and church, who never lost hope for me. I believe prayer drove away many evil spirits that often seemed to hover around me, especially in those first weeks.
>
> After months of hard-fought struggle, my bondage to evil was finally severed. Then came the unforgettable moment when the forgiveness of all my sins was spoken out by my pastor, in God's stead. The power and joy of that moment knew no bounds.

When we are burdened by sin, it is a tremendous gift to find someone to talk to about it. Pouring out one's heart to another person is like opening a sluice gate in a dam – the water runs out, and the pressure disappears. If confession is honest and heartfelt, it can bring a deep feeling of relief, because it is the first step on the road to forgiveness. But ultimately we have to stand before God. We cannot run away or hide from him, as Adam and Eve tried to do when they disobeyed him. If we are willing to stand before him in the light of his son Jesus, he will burn away all our guilt.

Just as God gave the first man and woman peace and joy in the Garden of Eden, he gives every believer the task of working toward the new order of his peaceable kingdom. To carry out this task, we must joyfully accept the rule of God in our lives and be willing to go the entire way of Jesus – to start at the stable in Bethlehem and end at the cross on Golgotha. It is a very lowly, humble walk. But it is the only way that leads to complete light and hope.

Jesus alone can forgive and remove our sins, because he alone is free from all stain. He can stir our consciences and set them free from impurity, bitterness, and discord (Heb. 9:14). If we accept the stirrings of our conscience, if we embrace God's judgment and mercy, it does not matter how sinful and corrupt we have been. In Christ the conscience that used to be our enemy becomes our friend.

Forgiveness has power to transform our lives.

The forgiveness of sins that Jesus offers is so powerful that it will change a person's life completely. Everything that makes us fearful or isolated, everything impure and deceitful, will yield if we give ourselves to him. What is up will come down, and what is down will come up. This change will start in the innermost heart of our being, and then both our inner and outer life, including all our relationships, will be transformed.

Whether or not a person has been transformed in this way shows up most plainly when he or she faces death. Those who have been at the bedside of a dying person will know how absolute, how final in its significance, is each person's inner relationship with God. They know that in the end, when the last breaths are drawn, this bond is the only thing that counts.

It is the life-task of every person to prepare to meet God. Jesus tells us how to do this when he says, "Whatever you do for the least of them you do to me." He also says, "Blessed are the poor in spirit, for theirs is the kingdom of God." I have personally experienced at deathbeds that if a person has lived for others, as Jesus did, then God is very close to him in the last hour. I have also experienced at the hour of death the torment of those who have lived selfish and sinful lives.

All of us, whether married or single, need to grasp more deeply the eternally healing words of Jesus: "Lo, I am with you always, even to the close of the age" (Matt. 28:20). In Jesus there is life, love, and light. In him our lives and our relationships can be purified from all that burdens us and opposes love, and God's image in us can be restored.

CHAPTER 6

Sexuality and the Sensuous Sphere

> Everything God created is good, and nothing is to be rejected if it is received with thanksgiving, because it is consecrated by the Word of God and prayer.
>
> *1 Timothy 4:4–5*

The Bible speaks of the heart as the center of a person's inner life. In the heart, decisions are made and the direction is set as to what spirit we will follow (Jer. 17:10). But God also created us as sensuous beings. To the sensuous belongs everything that we perceive with our senses, including sexual attraction. The scent of a flower, the warmth of the sun, or a baby's first smile brings us joy. God has given us a great gift in our senses, and if we use them to praise and honor him, they can bring us great happiness.

Yet just as the area of sensuous experience can bring us close to God, it can mislead us and even bring us into satanic darkness. All too often we tend toward the superficial and

* For chapters 6 and 7, the author acknowledges his indebtedness to Catholic philosopher Dietrich von Hildebrand (1889–1977), especially his book *Purity: The Mystery of Christian Sexuality*. See "For Further Reading."

miss the might and power of what God could otherwise give us. Too often, in grasping at what we experience with our senses, we forget about God and miss the possibility of experiencing the full depth of his will.

Lasting joy is found not in our senses, but in God.

To reject the living senses is to reject God and his handiwork (1 Tim. 4:1–3). The Spirit does not want us to reject the body or its emotional powers. But we should not forget that Satan seeks to undermine every good thing; he is a twister of the truth and is always waiting to deceive us, especially in this area.

Admittedly, the soul is drawn to God through the spirit, but it is always bound to the physical through the body. The physical is not the real enemy of the spirit, and it must never be despised. The real enemy is Satan, who continually tries to attack the human soul and sever it from God. God's will is that every part of life – spirit, soul, and body – be brought under his control for his service (1 Cor. 10:31).

In and of itself there is nothing wrong with the sphere of the senses. After all, everything we do, whether waking or sleeping, is a sensory experience at some level. But because we are not mere animals, because we are made in the image of God, far more is expected of us.

When two people fall in love, the joy they have at first is on a sensuous level: they look into each other's eyes, they hear one another speak, they rejoice in the touch of the other's hand, or even in the warmth of the other's closeness. Of course, the experience goes far deeper than seeing, hearing, or feeling, but it still begins as an experience of the senses.

Yet human love can never remain at this level – it must go much deeper than that. When the sensuous becomes an end in itself, everything seems fleeting and temporary, and we feel compelled to seek our satisfaction in experiences of greater and greater intensity (Eph. 4:17–19). Spending our energies on the intoxication of our senses, we soon exhaust and ruin our ability to take in life's vital power. And we also lose the capacity for any deep inner experiences. An acquaintance who has been married for over thirty years told me:

> When my wife and I first married, I always wanted her to dress smart and sexy. It was the heyday of the mini-skirt, and I thought she looked great in one. I did not recognize the damage this attitude did to her, to other men, and to myself. I was actually encouraging the lustful glance that Jesus so clearly denounces. Only later, when my wife and I realized this, did we find freedom from an unhealthy emphasis on each other's physical appearance and the way forward to a more genuine relationship.

Unless we surrender ourselves (including our senses) in reverence to God, we will be unable to experience the things of this world to their fullest. Time and again I have seen how people who focus on gratifying their senses wind up leading shallow, aimless lives. When our senses rule, we become frustrated and confused. But in God we can experience the eternal in the sensuous. In him we can satisfy our heart's deepest longings for what is genuine and lasting.

When we surrender our sexuality to God, it becomes a gift.

As a gift from God, sensuality is a mystery; without God, its mystery is lost and it is desecrated. This is especially true for the whole area of sex. The sexual life has a deep intimacy all its own, which each of us instinctively hides from others. Sex is each person's secret, something that affects and expresses one's innermost being. Every disclosure in this area opens up something intimate and personal and lets another person into one's secret. Therefore the sexual sphere – even though it is one of God's greatest gifts – is also the sphere of shame. We are ashamed to unveil our secret before others. There is a reason for this: just as Adam and Eve were ashamed of their nakedness before God because they knew that they had sinned, all of us know that we are sinful by nature. This recognition is not an unhealthy mental disorder, as many psychologists claim. It is the instinctive response to protect that which is holy and given by God, and it should lead every person to repentance.

Sexual union is meant to be the expression and fulfillment of an enduring and unbreakable bond of love. It represents the supreme surrender to another human being because it involves the mutual revelation of each partner's most intimate secret. To engage in sexual activity of any kind without being united in the bond of marriage, therefore, is a desecration. The widespread practice of premarital sexual "experimentation," even with a partner one intends to marry, is no less terrible, and it can severely damage a future marriage. The veil of intimacy between a man and woman must not be lifted without the blessing of God and the church in marriage (Heb. 13:4).

Even within a marriage, the whole sphere of sexual intimacy must be placed under Christ if it is to bear good fruit. The contrast between a marriage where Christ is in the center and one where the flesh is the focal point is best described by the Apostle Paul in his letter to the Galatians:

> The acts of the sinful nature are obvious: sexual immorality, impurity, and debauchery; idolatry and witchcraft; hatred, discord, jealousy, fits of rage, selfish ambition, dissension, factions, and envy; drunkenness, orgies, and the like. I warn you, as I did before, that those who live like this will not inherit the kingdom of God. But the fruit of the Spirit is love, joy, peace, patience, kindness, goodness, faithfulness, gentleness, and self-control. Against such things there is no law. Those who belong to Christ Jesus have crucified the sinful nature with its passions and desires (Gal. 5:19–24).

People who see sexual lust in the same way as they see gluttony do not understand the significance of the sexual sphere. When we surrender to the temptations of lust or sexual impurity, we are defiled in quite a different way than by gluttony, even though that, too, is condemned by Paul. Lust and impurity wound us in our innermost heart and being. They attack the soul at its core. Whenever we fall into sexual impurity, we fall prey to demonic evil, and our whole being is corrupted. Then only through deep repentance and conversion can we be freed.

The opposite of impurity is not legalism.

The opposite of sexual impurity and sensuality, however, is not prudery, moralism, or false piety. How seriously Jesus warns us against this! (Matt. 23:25–28) In everything we experience with our senses, our joy must be genuine and free. Pascal says, "The passions are most alive in those who want to renounce them." When sensuality is repressed by moral compulsion rather than disciplined from within, it will only find new channels of untruthfulness and perversity (Col. 2:21–23).

In our corrupt and shameless time, it is harder and harder to raise children with a deep sense of reverence for God and all that he has created. All the more, we must strive to bring up our children in such a way that whether or not they marry as adults, they grow up to be men and women committed to a life of purity.

We must be watchful that our children do not talk irreverently about sexual matters. Yet at the same time we cannot avoid the issue. Rather, we need to bring to our children a spirit of reverence. We must teach them to understand the significance and holiness of sex in God's order, and impress on them the importance of keeping their bodies pure and undefiled for the single purpose of marriage. They must learn to feel, as we do, that sex finds its greatest fulfillment, and therefore gives greatest pleasure, only in a pure and godly marriage.

God has joy when a young married couple experiences full uniting: first in spirit, then from heart to heart and soul to soul, and then in body. When a man and woman lift the veil of sex in reverence before him, in relationship with him, and in the unity given by him, their union honors God. Every couple should strive for this reverence, for "the pure in heart shall see God."

CHAPTER 7

The Pure in Heart

Blessed are the pure in heart, for they shall see God...Since we have these promises, dear friends, let us purify ourselves from everything that contaminates body and spirit, perfecting holiness out of reverence for God.

Matthew 5:8; 2 Corinthians 7:1

Søren Kierkegaard says that purity of heart is to will one thing. That one thing is God and his will. Apart from God, our hearts remain hopelessly divided. What is impurity, then? Impurity is separation from God. In the sexual sphere it is the misuse of sex, which occurs whenever sex is used in any way that is forbidden by him.

Impurity never pollutes us from without. It cannot be outwardly wiped away at will. Originating in our imagination, it breaks out from inside us like an infected sore (Matt. 15:16–20). An impure spirit is never satisfied, never whole: it always wants to steal something for itself, and even then lusts for still more. Impurity stains the soul, corrupts the conscience, destroys the coherence of life, and eventually leads to spiritual death.

An impure heart is neither satisfied nor free.

Whenever we allow our soul to be touched by impurity, we open it to a demonic force that has power to gain control over every sphere of our life, not only the sexual. Impurity can take the form of idolatrous passion for professional sports; it can be the ambitious craving for prestige or power over other people. If we are ruled by anything but Christ, we are living in impurity.

Impurity in the sexual sphere consists in using another person solely in order to satisfy desire. It is there wherever people enter into situations of sexual intimacy with no intention of forming a lasting bond.

One of the starkest forms of impurity occurs when a person engages in sexual intercourse (or any other sexual act) for the sake of money. A person who does this "becomes one with the harlot," as the Apostle Paul says, because he is using the body of another human being simply as a thing, a means of self-gratification. In doing this he commits a crime against the other person, but also against himself: "He who goes to the prostitute becomes the murderer of his own life" (1 Cor. 6:15–20). Even in marriage, sex for its own sake is sex separated from God. As von Hildebrand writes, it possesses a poisonous sweetness that paralyzes and destroys.

It would be a great mistake, however, to imagine that the opposite of impurity is the absence of sexual feeling. In fact, the lack of sexual awareness is not necessarily even fertile ground for purity. A person who lacks sensitivity to sex is in actual fact an incomplete person: he or she lacks something not only in natural disposition, but in that which gives color to his or her whole being.

People who seek purity do not despise sex. They are simply free from prudish fear and hypocritical shows of disgust. But they never lose reverence for the mystery of sex, and they will keep a respectful distance from it until they are called by God to enter its territory through marriage.

For unmarried Christians, suppression of sexual feelings is not the answer; only when they are surrendered completely to Christ will purity be found. In marriage, two people entrust the special holiness of the sexual area to each other. Yet in the deepest sense it is not they who give this gift to each other, but God, who created us all as sexual beings. Thus, whenever we give in to temptation – even if only in our thoughts – we are sinning against God, who created our sexuality for his purpose, which is the sanctity of marriage.

God wants to give inner harmony and decisive clarity to every heart. In this lies purity (James 4:8). As Eberhard Arnold writes:

> If one's heart is not clear and undivided – "single," as Jesus put it – then it will be weak, flabby, and indolent, incapable of accepting God's will, of making important decisions, and of taking strong action. That is why Jesus attached the greatest significance to singleness of heart, simplicity, unity, solidarity, and decisiveness. Purity of heart is nothing else than absolute integrity, which can overcome desires that enervate and divide. Determined single-heartedness is what the heart needs in order to be receptive, truthful and upright, confident and brave, firm and strong.[12]

The key to purity is humility.

In the Beatitudes Jesus blesses the pure and the meek; he says that they shall inherit the earth and see God. Purity and meekness belong together, because they both arise from complete surrender to God. In fact, they depend on it. But purity and meekness are not inborn; they must be struggled for again and again. There are few things more wonderful a Christian can strive for.

The struggle against sexual impurity is not just a problem for young adults. For many people, it does not lessen as they grow older and more mature but remains a serious struggle for life. Certainly a desire for purity is good and necessary, yet it remains impossible for anyone to "resolve" never to give in to temptation again. Only through the experience of forgiveness can the gift of purity be given. And even then, our battle against temptations will continue. Still, we can take courage. No matter how often or how sorely we are tempted, Jesus will plead to God on our behalf if we ask him. In him we will find victory over every temptation (1 Cor. 10:13).

Yet only the humble can experience God's infinite goodness. The proud never can. Proud people open their hearts to all sorts of evil: impurity, lying, stealing, and the spirit of murder. Where there is one of these sins, the others will not be far behind. People who strive for purity in their own strength will always be stumbling. Seemingly self-confident, they fall into darkness and sin because they think they can handle their problems on their own.

Each of us faces temptations in the sexual area, and our only hope in overcoming these lies in our willingness to confess our struggle to someone we trust. When we do this, we discover that we are by no means unique.

Frank, a young man who has shared with me about his struggle for purity, writes:

> Even as a small child, I considered myself to be a special and "spiritual" person. Once I established this image, I found it extremely difficult to share my problems with my parents or with anyone else. As I grew up, all my energy went into being a "good" boy. I would watch people I thought were "cool," and I would try to imitate them. This self-obsession continued during my college years. I chose to follow the crowd and drift along wherever the stream of college life took me.
>
> As I grew older, I saw my peers maturing into functional adults. Scared that I was being left behind, I refined my efforts to hide my deep insecurity, a problem that by now amounted to a mental disorder. Rather than look for suave role models, I turned to men who seemed to be spiritually gifted and tried to copy them.
>
> As the years went by, my fear that something might be chronically wrong with my life increased. Because of my pride, I was tormented and plagued by mistrust, doubts, and hatred. At the same time I led a secret life of sexual impurity. But I suppressed all this and lived in constant fear of being found out.

Too often I have watched people who could have been helped early on lose hope and slide further into sexual sin. Like an avalanche, their problems mount. Some even fall for a life of crime, drugs, and alcohol abuse simply because they see no way out. Often all such a person needs is a friend or pastor to point him toward God and encourage him to work for the purity he actually craves. (Frank eventually confronted his desperate need and asked for help.) A person's intense self-absorption, which is often camouflaged pride, shields him from the great promise that every temptation can be overcome – if only he is willing to admit his failings and turn away from himself.

Humble people, on the other hand, live in God's strength. They may fall, but God will always lift them up and rescue them from a downward spiral.

Of course, not only our struggles but everything in our lives should be placed under Jesus. Jesus overcomes the desires that tear us apart and dissipate our strength. The more firmly we are gripped by his Spirit, the nearer we will come to finding our true character.

Who is pure in heart?

In the Sermon on the Mount we can see how seriously Jesus takes the daily fight for purity. He says that if we look at another person with a lustful glance, we have already committed adultery in our hearts (Matt. 5:27–30). The fact that Jesus speaks about lustful thoughts – let alone lustful actions – should show us how important a decisive attitude of heart is in this fight.

Bonhoeffer writes, "Who is pure in heart? Only those who have surrendered their hearts completely to Jesus that he alone may remain in them; only those whose hearts are undefiled by their own evil – and by their own virtue as well."[13]

Pure men and women are able to discern both the good and the evil in the sexual sphere. They are awake to its intrinsic qualities and fully aware of its goodness and beauty as a gift from God. But they are also keenly aware that even the slightest misuse of this gift opens the door to evil spirits, and they know they cannot free themselves from these spirits in their own strength. That is why they avoid every situation that defiles the soul and abhor the thought of leading others into sin.

It is of vital importance that in our fight for purity we reject everything that belongs to the domain of sexual impurity, including greed, vanity, and every other form of self-indulgence. Our attitude cannot be one of "partial" fascination with lust – only one of complete rejection. If our hearts are pure, we will react instinctively against anything that threatens to cloud this attitude.

Here the church community has a great responsibility to fight daily for an atmosphere of purity among all of its members (Eph. 5:3–4). The fight for purity must go hand in hand with the fight for justice and community, because there is no true purity of heart without a feeling for justice (James 1:26–27). Purity is not just related to the sexual area; to know that a neighbor is hungry and to go to bed without giving him food is to defile one's heart. That is why the early Christians pooled everything they possessed – their food and drink, their goods, their strength, even their intellectual and creative activity – and gave them up to God. Because they were of one heart and soul and held all things in common, they could fight all things through to victory as one body.

Marriage is no guarantee of purity.

It is an illusion to think that the struggle for purity comes to an end as soon as one is married. Marriage can even be a trap. Many young people think that all their problems will be solved the minute they are married, but the fact is that many of their problems will only begin then.

Certainly, the union between husband and wife is a great grace. It can have a redeeming effect, especially in the sense of softening one's ego. But the redemptive effect of marriage can never be complete in itself. No one can ever solve the need of a partner's burdened conscience. Full redemption can be found only in Jesus.

A marriage certificate is no guarantee of purity. Whenever a true relationship to God is missing, sex quickly loses its true depth and dignity and becomes an end in itself. Even in marriage, superficiality in the sexual sphere spells ruin because it breaks down the mystery of the bond between man and woman.

It is tragic how so many today, even among Christians, use the marriage certificate as a license for satisfying every desire. A middle-aged couple I once met shared with me how, in the privacy of their own bedroom, they periodically watched pornographic videos to help "keep their love life alive." They saw nothing wrong with this. "Doesn't God want a couple to enjoy each other?" was their rationale. Little could they see how twisted and cheap their love life had become. Their attempts to substitute their lives with those of others only served to fuel their dissatisfaction with each other.

Nothing should reveal the need of God's special sanction more plainly than marriage. Therefore, whenever a man and woman unite, they should have the attitude Moses had when he came upon the burning bush: "Here is holy ground, take off your shoes!" (Exod. 3:5) Their attitude must always be one of reverence for their creator and for the mystery of marriage.

As the union of a husband and wife under God, sex fulfills its divinely ordained function in a profound way: it is tender, peaceful, and mysterious. Far from being an animal-like act of aggression and lust, it creates and expresses a unique bond of deep, self-giving love.

When a couple experiences the sexual sphere in this way, they will feel that their union cannot be meant only for procreation. At the same time, they must remember that through their uniting a new life may come into being. If they are truly reverent, they will feel such an awe for the holiness of this fact that their union will become like a prayer to God.

Without Christ, a man or woman who has lived in impurity cannot grasp the mysterious depth of the sexual sphere. But in Christ there can be complete healing. "For we know that when he appears, we shall be like him, for we shall see him as he is. Everyone who has this hope in him purifies himself, just as he is pure" (1 John 3:3).

What God Has Joined Together

CHAPTER 8

Marriage in the Holy Spirit

> I urge you to live a life worthy of the calling you have received. Be completely humble and gentle; be patient, bearing with one another in love. Make every effort to keep the unity of the Spirit through the bond of peace.
>
> *Ephesians 4:1–3*

Every marriage goes through tests and crises, but these can bring about an increase in love, and every young couple should remember this. True love provides the strength needed to meet every test. It means deeds, acts of helping one another in humble, mutual submission. True love is born of the Holy Spirit.

Often we overlook the depth of this truth. We tend either to dismiss true love as some sort of flimsy fairy tale or to focus so much energy on finding it that we miss it entirely. But the true love that stems from the Holy Spirit is not brought about by human effort. A married couple who experiences its blessings will notice their love increasing with each passing year, regardless of the trials they may encounter. Decades into their marriage, they will still find joy in making each other happy. As Jean, an acquaintance who has been married for over forty years, writes, expressions of love do not require much fanfare. Often the simplest gesture says the most.

> My husband, Chad, and I have gone through many struggles in our relationship with each other, and with our children. Yet through it all our love has grown stronger. Again and again we marvel at the gift God gave us in each other. I do not believe that our relationship could ever exist without romance – the little joys or surprises we make for each other are what confirm and renew our love time and again. I am always happily surprised when Chad, who is a writer, presents me with a poem or brings home flowers for our table. And how he loves it when I have a cup of coffee ready for him, or fresh-baked cookies, when he comes home from work at the end of the day.
>
> We have discovered that nothing is more reviving than a good laugh as we recount the day's little experiences to each other, or when he pulls my leg about something...It is true that marriage is a serious commitment for life, yet I think we can also be very childlike about it and trust in God's leading, taking one step at a time. We stumble along; we make our mistakes; we have our disagreements and arguments. But afterwards we love each other all the more.

The spirit opens up an entirely different plane of experience.

When two people seek a relationship, they usually do so in terms of mutual emotions, common values, shared ideas, and a feeling of good will toward each other. Without despising these, we must recognize that the Holy Spirit opens up an entirely different plane of experience between husband and wife.

Certainly, marital love based on the impulses of the emotions can be wonderful, but it can all too quickly become desperate and unhappy. In the long run it is an unstable foundation. Love gains certainty and firmness only when it is ruled by the Spirit.

If we seek only the unity and love that is possible on a human level, we remain like clouds drifting and suspended. When we seek unity in the Spirit, God can ignite in us a faithful love that can endure to the end. The Spirit burns away everything that cannot endure. He purifies our love. True love does not originate from ourselves, but is poured out over us.

Marriage in the Holy Spirit signifies faithfulness. Where there is no loyalty, there is no true love. In our society, marriages are being tested as never before, but this should refine and increase our faithfulness to one another. Faithfulness springs from the inward certainty of our calling. It comes from submission to God's order.

In his *Confession of Faith* (1540), the Anabaptist Peter Riedemann describes God's order for marriage as encompassing three levels. First is the marriage of God to his people, of Christ to his church, and of the Spirit to our spirit (1 Cor. 6:17). Second is the community of God's people among themselves – justice and common fellowship in spirit and soul. Third is the unity between one man and one woman (Eph. 5:31), which "is visible to and understandable by all."[14]

Unity of faith is the surest basis for marriage.

Paul the Apostle also draws a parallel between marriage and spiritual unity when he tells husbands to love their wives "just as Christ loved the church and gave himself up for her" (Eph. 5:25). For Christians, marriage is a reflection of the deepest unity: the unity of God and his church. In a Christian marriage, therefore, it is the unity of God's kingdom, in Christ, and in the Holy Spirit that matters most. Ultimately, it is the only sure foundation on which a marriage can be built. "Seek first God's kingdom and his justice, and all these things will be given to you as well" (Matt. 6:33).

Marriage should always lead two believing people closer to Jesus and his kingdom. It is not good enough for a couple to get married in a church or by a minister. To be drawn nearer to Christ, they must first be fully dedicated as individuals to the spirit of God's kingdom, and to the church community that serves it and stands under its direction. First there must be heart-felt unity of faith and spirit. Only then will there be true unity of soul and body as well.

This is why (at least traditionally) so many churches have been reluctant to bless the union of a member with a spouse who does not share his or her faith in Christ (2 Cor. 6:14). (In Ezra, chapters 9 and 10, we read how the prophet had to come before God and repent deeply on behalf of all the Israelites because they were marrying women from pagan nations.) On the one hand, they believe that anyone who is really drawn by the spirit of love and justice professed by a truly Christian church will not remain an "outsider"; on the other, they feel that a marriage between a member and a person who is not drawn to the life of the church and the basic premises of its beliefs would prevent both partners from finding the spiritual unity that is the highest level of marriage.

If, however, a person already married to someone of a different belief wished to join the church I pastor, I would do my utmost to preserve the marriage, as long as the new member did not feel hindered in faith by his or her spouse.

When the love of two people who desire to be married is dedicated to the Holy Spirit and placed under his rule and direction – when it serves the unity and justice of God's kingdom – there is no reason why the two should not marry. But when a couple lacks spiritual unity, marriage in the church should be out of the question. If the church is truly the Body, the unity of its members under God must come before everything else.

Here it should be said that the demands of a true marriage in the Spirit can never be met by a human system of answers or solved by means of principles, rules, and regulations. They can be grasped only in the light of unity, by those who have experienced the spirit of unity, accepted it personally, and begun to live in accordance with it.

The very essence of God's will is unity (John 17:20–23). It was God's will for unity that brought Pentecost to the world. Through the outpouring of the Spirit, people's hearts were struck, and they repented and were baptized. The fruits of their unity were not only spiritual. The material and practical aspects of their lives, too, were affected and even revolutionized. Goods were collected and sold, and the proceeds were laid at the feet of the apostles. Everyone wanted to give all they had out of love. Yet no one suffered want, and everyone received what he or she needed. Nothing was held back. There were no laws or principles to govern this revolution. Not even Jesus said exactly how it should be brought about, only, "Sell all you have and give it to the poor" (Matt. 19:21). At Pentecost it simply happened: the Spirit descended and united the hearts of those who believed (Acts 2:42–47).

The Spirit frees us from pettiness and brings unity of heart.

Genuine unity, like joy or love, cannot be forced or created artificially. Only the Spirit can bring unity. Only the Spirit can free us from our pettiness and from the forces of guilt and sin that divide us from God and from each other. With our own wills we can certainly try to free ourselves from these forces, and we may be able to overcome them to a certain degree and for a certain period of time. But we should remember that ultimately only the spirit of love can overcome the flesh.

Again, we must never forget our dependence on the guidance of the Holy Spirit (Gal. 5:25). Even within a marriage, if our unity is based only on mutual feelings or common values and not on the Spirit, it runs the risk of being swallowed up by the purely sexual and emotional. We ourselves are not capable of bringing about the true unity of spirit in which two hearts become one. That can happen only when we allow ourselves to be gripped and transformed by something greater than ourselves.

When a marriage is anchored in the Holy Spirit, both partners will feel that their love is not a private possession but a fruit and gift of God's uniting love. They may still struggle with selfishness, disunity, superficiality, or other disorders, but if they keep their hearts open, the Spirit will always lift their eyes to God and his help.

The Spirit must come to each of us, whether married or unmarried, again and again. It wants to transform everything in our hearts and give us the strength to love. In his

First Letter to the Corinthians, Paul says, "There is nothing love cannot face; there is no limit to its faith, its hope, and its endurance. Love will never come to an end." Love is born of the Holy Spirit, and only in the Spirit can a true marriage be conceived – and endure.

CHAPTER 9

The Mystery of Marriage

Submit to one another out of reverence for Christ. Wives, submit to your husbands as to the Lord. For the husband is the head of the wife as Christ is the head of the church, his body, of which he is the Savior. Now as the church submits to Christ, so also wives should submit to their husbands in everything. Husbands, love your wives, just as Christ loved the church and gave himself up for her to make her holy, cleansing her by the washing with water through the Word, and to present her to himself as a radiant church, without stain or wrinkle or any other blemish, but holy and blameless. In this same way, husbands ought to love their wives as their own bodies. He who loves his wife loves himself. After all, no one ever hates his own body, but he feeds and cares for it, just as Christ does the church, for we are members of his body. For this reason a man will leave his father and mother and be united to his wife, and the two will become one flesh. This is a profound mystery, but I am talking about Christ and the church.

Ephesians 5:21–32

In God's order, marriage and family originate in the church. The church is God's primary expression of his love and justice in the world. In the church, marriage can be fulfilled and given its true value. Without the church, it is doomed to be overcome by the dominating and destructive forces of society.

Marriage is more than a bond between husband and wife.

Only very few people in our day understand that marriage contains a mystery far deeper than the bond of husband and wife, that is, the eternal unity of Christ with his church. In a true marriage, the unity of husband and wife will reflect this deeper unity. It is not only a bond between one man and one woman, because it is sealed by the greater bond of unity with God and his people. This bond must always come first. It is this bond we pledge at baptism and reaffirm at every celebration of the Lord's Supper, and we should remind ourselves of it at every wedding. Without it, even the happiest marriage will bear no lasting fruit.

How little the marriage bond amounts to when it is only a promise or contract between two people! How different the state of the modern family would be if Christians everywhere were willing to place loyalty to Christ and his church above their marriages.

For those who have faith, Christ – the one who truly unites – always stands between the lover and the beloved. It is his Spirit that gives them unhindered access to one another. Therefore, when sin enters a marriage and clouds the truth of love, a faithful disciple will follow Jesus in the church, not his or her wayward partner.

Emotional love will protest this because it is prone to disregard the truth. It may even try to hinder the clear light that comes from God. It is unable and unwilling to let go of a relationship, even when it becomes false and ungenuine. But true love never follows evil: it rejoices in the truth (1 Cor. 13:6). Both partners must recognize that unity of faith is more important than the emotional bond of their marriage. Each of us who claims to be a disciple must ask ourselves: "If my first allegiance is not to Jesus and the church, who is it to?" (Luke 9:57–60)

When the smaller unity of a married couple is placed under the greater unity of the church, their marriage becomes steadfast and secure on a new, deeper level because it is placed within the unity of all believers. It is hardly surprising that this idea is foreign to most people, yet it contains a truth I have witnessed time and again. Take the story of Harry and Betty, an elderly couple I got to know well during their last years together. In Betty's words:

> Harry and I were married in June 1937, in England. Though at first we felt our marriage to be founded under God, it was not long before our struggles began. Harry, who struggled with homosexual inclinations all his life, became unfaithful to me, and then left me. Several times he tried to set things straight, but he never seemed to be able to break with the sin that bound him. During our long years of separation, close friends stood by him and me, and this was a great support.
>
> When distressing letters came from Harry, I got discouraged, and sometimes I gave up praying for him. But I always came back to it, as it was the only thing I could do to help him. I knew that with God everything is possible, and hoped that someday Harry might be restored to Christ and the church…
>
> Now I can never cease to marvel at what a miracle it was that he returned to me in his old age. We had not been

> together for over forty years. But I loved being with him during the last years we shared; he was so different. He was humble and straightforward and childlike. He came to love my friends, and our neighbors, and they loved him. Harry and I read the Bible and his favorite hymns together. He was very close to Jesus in his final months.
>
> I think of him every day and will always treasure the time I had with him. I think he was closer to the kingdom than I am. I fail in love again and again and see too late things I could have done. But God is faithful and keeps his promises. My faith rests in this, and I have peace.

Betty was too modest to ever say it, but had it not been for her constant prayer and her faithfulness to Jesus, Harry might never have found his way back to God and to faith in Him, let alone back to her. Their last two years together are a testament to faith and to the healing power of uncompromising love. What a contrast to today's culture, where so many seem to think that the more independently a marriage is built, the firmer it is. Some even think that the more a couple can be relieved of the "constraints" of obligation to each other, the happier they will be. This is a completely false presumption. Only when a marriage is founded in God's order and on the basis of his love can it last. A marriage is built on sand unless it is built on the rock of faith.

Man and woman have different tasks, and they must complement each other.

The belief that love to Christ and his church must take priority over all else is also important for understanding the difference between man and woman. Clearly God has given each of them different natures and tasks, and when these are rightly fulfilled in a marriage in the church, harmony and love will abound. My father, J. Heinrich Arnold, writes:

> Obviously, there are differences in the biological makeup of the male and the female. But it is completely materialistic to think that the difference between man and woman is merely biological. A woman longs to absorb her beloved one into herself. She is designed by nature to receive and to endure; to conceive, to bear, to nurse, and to protect. A man, on the other hand, desires to enter his beloved one and become one with her; he is made to initiate and penetrate rather than to receive.[15]

It has been said that the body is shaped by the soul, and this is a deep thought. The soul, the breath of God, the innermost essence of each human being, forms a different body for each. It is never a question of who is higher. Both man and woman were made in the image of God, and what can be greater than that? Yet there is a difference: Paul likens man to Christ and woman to the church (Eph. 5:22–24). Man, as Head, portrays the service of Christ. Woman, as Body, portrays the dedication of the church. There is a difference in calling, but there is no difference in worth.

Mary is a symbol of the church. In her we recognize the true nature of womanhood and motherhood. Woman is like the church because she receives and carries the Word within her (Luke 1:38) and brings life into the world in keeping with God's will. This is the highest thing that can be said of a human being.

A woman's love is different from a man's. It is more steady, more in keeping with her loyal nature. It is dedicated to protecting and guiding all those in its care. Man's love, on the other hand, seeks others out and challenges them. It is the pioneering love of the apostle, of Christ's representative: "Go out and gather! Teach all people. Submerge them in the atmosphere of God, in the life of God the Father, the Son, and the Holy Spirit" (Matt. 28:18–20). But man's task, like woman's, is always bound together with the task of the church.

Both Paul and Peter point out that man is the head of woman, not in himself but in Christ (1 Cor. 11:3). This does not mean that the man is "higher"; the fact that woman is taken from man and man is born of woman shows that they are dependent on each other in every respect (1 Cor. 11:11–12). Again, the gifts and responsibilities of one are worth no more than those of the other; they are simply different. In the true order of marriage, both husband and wife will find their rightful place, but neither will rule the other. Love and humility will rule.

It belongs to the evil of our day that both men and women avoid the responsibilities given them by God. Women rebel against the inconvenience of pregnancy and the pain of birth, and men rebel against the burden of commitment to the children they father and to the woman who bears them. Such rebellion is a curse on our time. It will lead future generations astray. Woman was designed by God to have children, and a true man will respect and love his wife all the more because of this. Peter admonishes us:

> You husbands must conduct your married life with understanding: pay honor to the woman's body, not only because it is weaker, but also because you share together in the grace of God which gives you life. Then your prayers will not be hindered (1 Pet. 3:7).

It is clear that the difference between man and woman is not absolute. In a true woman there is courageous manliness, and in a true man there is the submission and humility of Mary. Yet because the man is the head, in a true marriage he will give the lead, even if he is a very weak person. This must not be taken as if man were an overlord and woman his servant. If a man does not lead in love and humility – if he does not lead in the spirit of Jesus – his headship will become tyranny. The head has its place in the body, but it does not dominate.

At weddings in our Bruderhof communities the bridegroom is always asked if he is willing to lead his wife "in everything that is good," which simply means to lead her more deeply to Jesus. In the same way, the bride is asked if she is willing to follow her husband. It is simply a matter of both of them following Jesus together.

True leadership means loving service.

In his letter to the Ephesians, Paul points to the self-sacrificing love that lies in true leadership: "Husbands, love your wives, just as Christ loved the church and gave himself up for her" (Eph. 5:25). This task, the task of loving, is actually the task of every man and woman, whether married or not.

When we take Paul's words to heart, we will experience the true inner unity of a relationship ruled by love – an inner speaking of the heart to God from both partners together. Only then will God's blessing rest on our marriages. We will constantly seek our beloved one anew and continually look for ways to serve each other in love. Most wonderful of all, we will find everlasting joy. As the church father Tertullian writes:

Who can describe the happiness of a marriage contracted in the presence of the church and sealed with its blessing? What a sweet yoke it is which here joins two believing people in one hope, one way of life, one vow of loyalty, and one service to God! They are brother and sister, both busy in the same service, with no separation of soul and body, but as two in one flesh. And where there is one flesh, there is one spirit also. Together they pray, together they kneel down: the one teaches the other, and bears with the other. They are joined together in the church of God, joined at the Lord's table, joined in anxiety, persecution, and recovery. They vie with each other in the service of their Lord. Christ sees and hears, and joyfully does he send them his peace, for where two are gathered together in his name, there is he in the midst of them.[16]

CHAPTER 10

The Sacredness of Sex

Marriage should be honored by all, and the marriage bed kept pure, for God will judge the adulterer and all the sexually immoral.

Hebrews 13:4

There are two dangers in sex: on the one hand, fear of the self-surrender or closeness that a physical relationship requires, and fear that sex is dirty and shameful; on the other, unbridled lust and sin. Clearly, the sexual sphere is not incorruptible. Even in marriage its potential blessings become dangers if it is entered in isolation from God, who created it. Instead of passion there is naked lust, instead of tenderness there is aggression and even brutality, and instead of mutual self-giving there is uncontrollable desire.

The church should never be silent about this (1 Cor. 5:1–5). The spirit of impurity is always waiting to tempt us, and it will slip into the sanctuary of marriage whenever we open the door to it. Once impurity has entered a marriage, it becomes more and more difficult to keep focused on God's love, and easier and easier to bypass one another and succumb to evil temptations.

We must never underestimate the power of the impure spirits that drive people to do evil, even within marriage.

Once under their control, sex quickly loses its nobler qualities and deteriorates into something cheap. What was created as a wonderful gift from God becomes a sinister, life-destroying experience. Only repentance can bring about healing and restoration.

**Through the marriage act,
an unparalleled uniting can take place.**

We can recognize the true nature of the sexual sphere most clearly when we can see its sacredness as the fulfillment of wedded love sanctioned by God. It is the same with the act of sexual intercourse itself, the moment in which marital love comes to its fullest physical expression. Because intercourse is such a powerfully dramatic experience, it is vital that it be anchored in God. If sex is not recognized as a gift from God and subordinated to him, it can become an idol. Entered with reverence, however, it "awakens that which is most intimate, most sacred, most vulnerable in the human heart."[17]

In a true marriage, sex is guided by more than the desires of each partner: it is guided by the love that binds both partners together. When each partner gives himself in complete surrender to the other, a uniting of unparalleled depth takes place. It will not be just "physical love"; it will be the expression and fulfillment of total love, an act of unconditional giving and deep fulfillment.

It is a remarkable and wonderful experience to give oneself physically to another person. Orgasm, the climax or peak of physical uniting, is a powerful and shaking experience and has a forceful effect on the spirit. Here, the experience of the body is so forceful that it is difficult to distinguish it from the experience of the spirit. In rhythmic harmony of heart and body, two human beings reach the highest peak of the joy of love. In total union, both are lifted out of their own personalities and joined in the closest community possible. At the moment of climax a person is, so to speak, swept away – engulfed so completely that the sense of being an independent person is momentarily submerged.

Physical union should always express unity of heart and soul.

We can never have too much reverence for the marriage act. Even if we reject prudishness, a feeling of reticence will make us wary of speaking about it to others. Of course, a man and woman united in marriage must be able to talk openly with each other, even about the most intimate things. But they will never do this without the reverence that springs from their love for each other.

It is of prime importance that a couple does not go to bed at night without having turned first to Jesus. It is not necessary to use many words; Jesus always knows what we mean and what we need. We must not only thank him but also seek his guidance – if we do not knock at his door, he cannot guide us. The same, of course, is true at the start of the day.

If our marriage is grounded in Jesus and his love and purity, we will find the right relationship to each other on every level. Here we must heed Paul's warning, "If you are angry, do not let your anger lead you into sin; do not let the sun go down on your anger, and do not give a foothold to the devil" (Eph. 4:26–27). Prayer is crucial in reconciling the differences that arise in the marriage relationship. To unite physically when there is no unity of spirit is hypocrisy. It is a desecration of the bond of love.

Physical uniting should always express the full uniting of spirit and soul; it should never be a means of bodily satisfaction alone. In Jesus, every physical act of love is a mutual giving of self, a sign of resolve to live for one another. It has nothing to do with power or the idea of sex as conquest.

Anyone who uses his partner merely to satisfy himself insults his own dignity and the dignity of his partner. He is using sex for a selfish purpose. This is why the Bible regards it as sin when a man withdraws from his wife before climax and allows his semen to "fall on the earth" (Gen. 38:9–10). Of course, if this happens against his will, prematurely, or in a dream, then it is not a sin. For the same reason, oral and anal intercourse are also sinful. Because they are driven only by the selfish desire for sexual excitement, these forms of sex are in reality forms of mutual masturbation.

True sexual fulfillment is found in mutual submission.

Sexual desire may be relatively dormant in a newly married couple, especially when neither partner has engaged in premarital sex or been addicted to masturbation. In fact, a husband may even need to awaken the urge for intercourse in his bride. Because this may take time, he should be very patient and initiate sexual union only when his wife is ready. For a virgin, the first intercourse can be painful and may cause minor bleeding. This is no cause for alarm, yet a husband should be aware of his wife's discomfort.

A true husband will have enough love for his wife to consider her state of readiness and not hurry intercourse because of his own impatience. Because he is concerned not merely with his own satisfaction, he will be sensitive to the fact that often more time is needed for a woman to reach climax than for a man, and after intercourse, he will not go happily to sleep while his wife lies awake with feelings of deep disappointment or frustration.

The sexual happiness of a woman is often more dependent than a man's on the accompanying circumstances of their union; on the unity she feels between herself and her husband, and in little acts of kindness or affectionate words. It does not consist only in the climax. Simply being together with her beloved may give her the deepest sense of fulfillment.

A couple should not be afraid to prepare one another for physical union. Loving stimulation is a strong affirmation of mutual unity, and in addition to increasing readiness, it nurtures confidence and envelops a couple with a feeling of security. Both husband and wife must learn what pleases and stimulates their partner. Writing about women, for instance, von Gagern says, "There are areas of the body that are especially responsive to fondling – the mouth, the breasts, under the arms, the spine – but a couple's own unique love for each other will continually guide them anew."[18]

As self-discipline, abstinence can deepen a couple's love.

Physically, intercourse is always possible, but a husband should be ready to abstain for the sake of his wife's health, especially before and after she gives birth. As a marriage counselor I have always recommended abstinence during menstruation and for at least six weeks before the birth of a child. I also recommend that couples abstain as long as they are able after a birth, so that the mother can recover both physically and emotionally. Because every couple is different, it is hard to suggest a time frame; the important thing is consideration. If a husband is truly considerate of his wife, he will be willing to discipline himself by abstaining as long as possible (1 Thess. 4:3–5). In such times of abstinence, out of love for her husband, the woman must be careful not to arouse him sexually.

Naturally, the love between man and wife – between two who live together, sleep together, and belong together – will make it much harder for them to abstain than for a single person. All the more, they must be on guard against coming close to one another in a sexual way and then avoiding intercourse.

One unfounded but prevalent idea is that abstinence must be fundamentally negative or frustrating. If born out of love, it can actually create a deeper, more enriching relationship. It can even have a healing affect. John Kippley, the director of a national ministry to couples, tells how a woman he knows who was abused by her father experienced healing through her husband's consideration of her needs. "Because of his restraint," she told John, "I was able to discover for the first time that I was more than my body. I could be loved without having to perform sexually. I had true value as a person, not just as an object of satisfaction."

As a woman approaches middle-age, it is not unusual for her joy or interest in sexual intercourse to diminish. This can be hard for the man, yet he must see that his love for his wife does not decrease. Wives, for their part, should give themselves in love to their husbands as they are able, even if their joy in doing so is not the same as it was in earlier years (1 Cor. 7:3–4). Otherwise a husband may be tempted to seek other outlets for his sexual impulses. The main thing is that there is always unity of spirit and soul before physical uniting and that, when abstinence is necessary, it does not become an occasion for love to grow cold. Paul writes:

> Do not deprive each other except by mutual consent and for a time, so that you may devote yourselves to prayer. Then come together again so that Satan will not tempt you because of your lack of self-control (1 Cor. 7:5).

Abstinence, then, may be best approached with fasting and prayer – as a self-discipline. When willingly accepted in this way, it can unite a couple more deeply than ever.

In the end, everything in a marriage depends on the commitment of both partners to Jesus and on their willingness to follow his leading. Couples should remember that it was God who joined them together, and only he can keep them together, especially in difficult times. Jesus says, "Whoever loses his life will gain it" (Luke 9:24). The same is true in Christian marriage: insofar as both partners are willing to surrender themselves again and again to each other and to Christ, they will find the true fulfillment of unity and freedom.

Parenthood and the Gift of Children

Children, obey your parents in the Lord, for this is right. "Honor your father and mother so that it may go well with you and so that you may enjoy long life on the earth." Fathers, do not exasperate your children; instead, bring them up in the training and instruction of the Lord.

Ephesians 6:1–4

We live in a world where the structure of family life is undergoing profound changes, in rich and poor countries alike. The concept of family as a stable, cohesive unit is fast becoming outdated. We are even afraid to define what a family is because we do not want to offend anyone.

For years, psychologists have warned of the effects of broken marriages, teen pregnancies, violent homes, and other social ills, but their warnings have been given in vain. Now we are reaping a bitter harvest. All this makes it more urgent than ever for us to rediscover God's original intent in creating man and woman, and in blessing them with children.[19]

Having children today requires courage.

Modern society despises the family. It is difficult for a family with several children to find a house, and in many places it is impossible to rent an apartment, even if there is only one child. Children are simply not wanted. Many people think it regrettable to leave jobs or other pursuits to have children, and they often look down on women who choose to stay at home to raise children instead of pursuing a more "acceptable" career.

Having children in these times certainly takes great courage, but that is what faith means: not knowing what lies ahead, and yet still trusting that God has his hand over all things and will have the final say. More than ever, parents need to trust God. The health of a society (and the health of any church or movement within society) depends on the strength of its marriages. Where there is reverence for God, there are strong and stable families, but as soon as this is lost, there is rapid disintegration and decline.

Those who know what it means to see a child smile for the first time, to love him or her, and to feel love in return know something of the greatness of God and the nearness of eternity in each child. They know that their child is like no other, and that no child could replace this one in their hearts. They will also realize what an awe-inspiring responsibility it is to bring a child into the world – a responsibility that only grows with the child – and will sense that they are too weak and sinful to bring up even one child in their own strength.

But our recognition of inadequacy should not lead us to despair. It should make us realize how dependent we are on grace. Only the adult who stands like a child before the grace of God is fit to raise a child.

On what basis should a family be built?

If we think of starting a family, our first question should be: on what foundation? Complete dedication to Christ and his church is the only dependable foundation. On him alone can we build a rich and fulfilled family life that will withstand the forces that attack it from outside.

It is the task of every couple to bring up their children on God's behalf, to represent the creator. For the small child especially, father and mother stand for God. That is why the commandment to honor father and mother is so vital to the upbringing of every child from the start. Without it, the commandment to honor God has no real meaning. Actually, every child has an instinctive longing for the security of father, mother, and God. It is terrible, then, when parents do not fulfill this longing, when they see parenting merely as a role and are not truly fathers or mothers. Children will sense such hypocrisy wherever it occurs, and they will become resentful, bitter, and rebellious as they grow older.

The same is true if a couple lives in dissension – if a woman does not support her husband's task as head of the family, for example, or if a man does not love and honor his wife. When children cannot find a picture of God in their parents, they have trouble finding a secure and healthy foundation for their later lives. They may even experience emotional difficulties.

Recently I counseled a family I have known since their four children were very young. The parents had all the right intentions, yet they were divided over whose role it was to lead the family. While visitors and outsiders were presented with a peaceful enough picture, within the family tensions and rivalry developed. As their children grew up, the parents were too disunited to lead them properly, and thereby set a poor example for them to follow.

Now their children are adults. They are all lovable, bright, and talented, yet they are floundering. Because their parents never dealt with the elements of mistrust and disunity in their marriage, these young adults now find it very hard to trust anyone. Like their parents, it is difficult for them to be sincere and honest with themselves, and they always need to feel in control. Sadly, they don't realize how this cuts them off from other people, and they have become lonely and disillusioned. Worst of all, they are wholly unrealistic in their expectations and seem to think the world owes them success.

It is of greatest importance that from the first day of a child's life he or she is surrounded by love and by reverence for God. To the same degree that children experience the love their parents have for each other, they will find the inner security they need in order to develop and grow.

In questions of discipline, it is best if a husband and wife are fully agreed as to what they expect in terms of behavior. Children should not have to decide which parent is right. Their position should be one of trust, not judgment. They look for consistent boundaries and for the security that comes from unity, love, and mutual respect. These things are the basis of true love for children.

Children need living examples,
not religious words.

The first five years of a child's life are formative, and therefore the best time for parents to bring Jesus and the gospel alive to their children. This can be done quite simply by telling them about Jesus' birth, death, and resurrection. All these things can move the hearts of children at a surprisingly young age and awaken in them a love for God and for Jesus.

We cannot bring our children to Jesus, however, if he is only a figure in our Bibles. Children will always want to come to Jesus, but they will instinctively rebel against false piety. As Blumhardt once put it, "If we try to drag children into the kingdom by means of our religiosity, they will flee from our pious homes as fast as they are able."[20] Therefore we should be careful not to put our children under any religious pressure or plague them with talk about sins they can neither understand nor commit. We want them to have a childlike attitude toward God, toward Jesus, and toward the Bible. It is of no use, for instance, to make children learn even the shortest passages of Scripture if God does not speak directly into their little hearts. Rather than try to "teach" children faith, it is much better for their parents to live their faith by example in a spontaneous, genuine way. When our children see that we, their parents, rely on God for everything – when they see us thank him and obey his commands – they will feel an inner urge to pray and to follow him of their own accord.

Our task is to guide our children, not control them.

Raising children requires daily discipline, but we should never forget that caring for them in God's stead means guiding, not controlling, them. Children must be encouraged to overcome themselves and look beyond their little worlds from a very early age, and they must learn to love and respect others. They cannot be left to swing with every mood and follow every selfish whim without restraint. Clear directions and consistent boundaries are always necessary. In fact, discipline is the greatest love we can show them (Heb. 12:10–11). But it is never loving to coerce or crush them.

We must remember that every child is a thought of God (Ps. 139:13–17) and try to understand why it is said that "a little child will lead them" (Isa. 11:6). In guiding our children, we cannot and should not try to shape them according to our own intentions or plans. We should not force on them anything that has not been born into them, awakened from within, or given them by God. God has a specific intent for each child; he has a plan for every one, and he will hold to it. Our task is to help each child find God's purpose for him and fulfill it.

Carrying out this task means continually exercising self-denial in our own human efforts to lead a child. Sometimes, it may mean refraining from tearing children away from their own thoughts. Blumhardt notes how quickly we hurt our relationship with children when we interrupt their thoughts and happy disposition and attempt to influence them by our ideas or advice: "When left undisturbed, children learn obedience and respect best of all."[21]

Naturally, we must be on guard against permissiveness. Flabbiness is often a fruit of an unhealthy emotionalism between parent and child. It inhibits the childlike spirit because it subjects the child to the spinelessness of an adult who has lost the clarity of Christ. We must always watch that our children are free from such false ties.

True authority strengthens and stimulates a child.

Children must never feel ill-used if spoken to or admonished sharply. They need to learn to take themselves in hand and face up to what has happened when they are shown to be in the wrong. They should not give half-answers that could mean this or that. Yet even if a certain sharpness toward children is healthy, impatience is not, especially when it results in corporal punishment. That, Eberhard Arnold writes, is a "declaration of bankruptcy."

We reject both the harshness of physical punishment and the power of manipulation: both are forms of authoritarianism that fail to take the child seriously as a bearer of God's image. The one fails in mercy, and the other in honesty. Both fail in love. True authority stimulates and strengthens what is good in each child by leading him to make his own decisions between right and wrong. Only when we lead children by trusting them and loving them will they feel the desire to struggle against the evil that tries to work in them and in each of us.

I thank God that I had a father who could be very strict with us children when necessary. Like any child, I rebelled at times against his strictness, but I always knew it was a sign of his love for me. From early childhood on, our parents instilled in us children the value of the fifth commandment, to honor father and mother. We knew that if we did not love and honor them, we were actually dishonoring God.

As for my mother, my father insisted that we children show her respect. He would not tolerate disobedience to her. Only in later years did I realize his wisdom. It is the father's task to uphold respect toward the mother, since she carries the weightier burden in raising their children, especially when they are small and sick.

Though my father could be stern, I never once felt threatened by him. Whenever he reprimanded me for doing something wrong, I could count on his complete forgiveness and love once I had accepted my responsibility and wanted to make amends. I knew that the wrong I had done would be forgotten, and that I would be able to make a fresh start.

My father showed me the significance of loving authority, an authority that only God can give. In each child's heart is a longing to hear a "no" when a "no" is needed, and a desire to set things right when he knows he has done something wrong. True parental authority gives inner security to a child, because it provides the child with the stability of set boundaries.

Most fathers and mothers do not intentionally mislead their children, and when they do mislead them without meaning to, they are no less likely to suffer the consequences then their children. Some parents are confident about their child-rearing abilities, and others are not, but there are times when both will throw up hands. When this is the case, it is vital that they find the humility to ask someone for help – whether a close friend, relative, a teacher, or a trusted pastor or family counselor. Of course, such help must be enlisted in such a way that it reassures the child in question – and not at the expense of a relationship with him or her. It is vital to remember that even the best expert assistance may, at the end of the day, be a hindrance – not a help. I say this because ultimately, "successful" parenting is not a matter of capability or wisdom, but of grace. My father writes in this regard:

> Christ calls us to become like children, and this means we must drop everything and become completely dependent on God and on one another. If we as parents love God with all our heart and soul, our children will have the right reverence for us, and we will also have reverence for our children and for the wonderful mystery of becoming and being a child. Reverence for the spirit that moves between parent and child is the basic element of a happy family life.[22]

CHAPTER 12

The Purity of Childhood

Whoever becomes humble like this child is the greatest in the kingdom of heaven. Whoever welcomes one such child in my name welcomes me. If any of you put a stumbling block before one of these little ones who believes in me, it would be better for you if a great millstone were fastened around your neck and you were drowned in the depth of the sea.

Matthew 18:4–6

Jesus' words tell us what great value the soul of a little child has in the eyes of God. Spiritually, every child is close to the throne of God, to the heart of God, and every child has a guardian angel who "always sees the face of the Father in heaven" (Matt. 18:10).

When a baby comes into the world it is as though he or she brings the pure air of heaven along. At every birth we feel that something of God is born, that something of eternity has come down to us. The innocence of a child is an enormous blessing.

The childlike spirit must be protected – but also nurtured.

In spite of the innocence of every child, however, there is also an inclination to sin in each one (Prov. 22:15). That is why it is such a terrible sin to lead a child astray. Children are corrupted not only by intentionally misleading them to sin, but by exposing them to anything that violates the atmosphere of innocence around them and deprives them of their childlikeness. So many of the images to which children are exposed today – at home on television, at shopping malls, and at school – are created by adults obsessed with sex, violence, power, and money. Is it any wonder that they lose their childlike spirit and childhood itself while they are still children?

The best thing we can do for our children is to see that the whole atmosphere in which they live is filled with the spirit of purity and ruled by love. The inner education of children – the task of leading them to respect and to love God, their parents, their teachers, and everyone around them – is a holy privilege. Here it is of utmost importance that we pray for God's spirit to arouse our children's wills for what is pure, genuine, and good. Guiding children to do what is good is far more important than teaching them to recite verses or to say prayers which may not come from the heart. That is why my church avoids formal religious instruction as such. We feel that children can learn to love God best through simple songs and through stories from the Bible, and through the daily example of adults around them who love each other.

In leading children to Jesus it is important that we ourselves have a childlike attitude toward his commandments and sayings, toward the angel-world, and toward the Bible as a whole. How very quickly and simply children take these things into their hearts!

We can also bring our children to God through the world around them, by helping them to sense him in all they see – in sun, moon, and stars; birds and animals; trees and flowers; mountains and thunderstorms. Every child wants to live in nature and with nature, and in every child there is a love for the earth, a joy in the starry sky, and a warm fondness for everything living. To a child, the world of God and his angels is often much closer and more real than we suspect.

Through nature and through the Bible, children will encounter suffering and death at an early age. While it is important for us to teach them to have a heart for those who suffer, it is equally important not to burden or frighten them. In general, too many facts about the cycle of life – of reproduction, birth, and death – can harm a child's inner experience of God's world. Birth and death are mysteries that can only be understood in relationship to God, and there is danger of irreverence in saying to much.

In this respect, we need to have a greater awe and reverence for pregnancy and childbirth. It is not without reason that Jesus compares the end times and the coming of a new world with a mother in labor, and the tremendous joy of the new life after all the pain and agony. Whenever a couple is expecting a child, a deep mystery is present. We can do great inward harm whenever we joke about pregnancy or draw too much attention to it. A quiet, humble anticipation will instill a natural reverence in children for God's gift of new life.

Concerning sex, especially, it is simply not necessary for a child or even an adolescent to know everything. It is all too easy to destroy our children's sense of the sacredness and mystery of life with too much discussion and exposure. Today as never before, parents must be alert to the insidious dangers of our sex-crazed culture, which can all too easily infiltrate our homes – through what we and our children see, hear, and read.

I am not in any way suggesting that children be brought up ignorant of the basic facts of life. I only mean that these things should never be separated from the world of God. The main thing is that we do not disturb the purity of childhood – the natural relationship of every child to his or her creator.

Education means rousing a child to choose right over wrong.

To protect the purity of children means to win them for the good. It is wrong to suppose that a child is not tempted to evil. As parents we must always be ready to fight evil in our children, whether it takes the form of lying, stealing, disrespect, or sexual impurity. But we must do this without too many rules (Col. 2:20–22). Moralism, which always involves suspicion and mistrust, ruins the childlike spirit. Obedience is never enough. Compliance alone does not build a child's character. On the one hand, children cannot be left unprotected to fall prey to whatever evil comes their way. On the other hand, we should not discourage them by constantly haranguing them about their faults. True education does not mean molding or squelching a child with constant criticism. It means rousing him or her to choose right over wrong.

Even from a very early age, we must be careful not to spoil our children. Spoiling leads to selfishness, lack of self-control, and deep discontent; in other words, it leads to sin. Parents who spoil their children often confuse love with emotionalism. They think they will win their children by clinging to them, but in actual fact they only hinder them from developing into healthy, independent beings. To treat one's children as one's emotional property is to lack reverence for them as images of God in their own right.

Among older children, disrespect toward peers, educators, and parents is not uncommon. Disrespect shows itself in many ways. Among boys it may take the form of machismo (which is mostly a cover-up for cowardice, and is only displayed when others are present) or a lack of consideration for others, or irreverent or destructive behavior. Singing may be despised as effeminate, signs of affection to babies may be scoffed at, and everything religious or moral is apt to be mocked. Among girls disrespect often shows itself in cruel gossip or backbiting, secrecy, and over-sensitivity to criticism.

Because children who demonstrate such tendencies are insecure, they are susceptible to peer pressure and will often turn to the support of a clique. Parents and teachers need to be alert to this, because the exclusive nature of even the friendliest clique is never healthy. The best antidote to cliquishness is positive guidance, care, and genuine interest in each child.

Every child instinctively longs for a good conscience.

The question of sexual impurity in children needs special sensitivity and discernment. My father writes:

How to fight against sin in children is a very difficult question. If there are indecencies, for example, which mostly begin with children exposing themselves to each other and sometimes touching each other, the child will feel instinctively that this is not right. These indecencies almost always involve lying. We must be careful not to make too much of such things among children. It may only draw their attention to the sexual area all the more. The best thing, perhaps, is to admonish them and so close the matter, and then help them to think of other things.

We grown-ups too easily forget that many things do not mean the same to a child as they do to us, and we must never project our ideas and feelings and experiences onto a child's mind (Titus 1:15). We must also never forget that it is in a certain way natural for children to go through periods of sexual curiosity. This cannot be mistaken for sin. But we should lead our children in such a way that their souls remain pure and innocent. Too much questioning can harm a child, because through fear he or she may become more and more entangled in lies.

It is a great injustice to label children or adolescents, especially those who have offended in the sexual area. In our assessment of childish offenses, we should beware of coming too quickly to harsh conclusions about a child's character or future development. Rather, we should help him or her to find new interests and to make a joyful new beginning.

We know that we can find the way to the heart of any child by appealing to the conscience. Every child has an instinctive, heartfelt longing for a pure conscience, and we should support this longing so that he or she does not suffer from a burdened conscience.

There is a certain point at which children are no longer children in the true sense of the word. The moment they sin consciously, they cease to be children. It is then the task of parents and teachers to help them find repentance, the experience of Jesus on the cross, and a conversion that leads to the forgiveness of sins. Through the cross a lost childhood can be restored.[23]

**Purity, like impurity,
is learned by example.**

For parents, the importance of seeking a relationship of trust with their children from earliest childhood cannot be emphasized enough. We cannot wait for problems that may only arise around the age of five or six. If we do not build relationships with our children while they are still young, we may never gain the trust and respect necessary to solve the more serious problems that will come with adolescence.

The years between thirteen and twenty-one are especially crucial, of course, since it is during these years that children become increasingly aware of their sexuality. How easy it is for parents – and whole churches – to turn a blind eye to the teenagers right in front of them and to fail them miserably simply by ignoring them. How different our American high schools would be if parents took time for their teenagers! Plenty of parents warn them about alcohol, drugs, and sexual experimentation, but how many take time on a regular basis to guide their children's interests and encourage them to use their time creatively, to do more than watch the latest videos or hang out at the mall? Committed parents will remain in close contact with their children throughout the ups and downs of adolescence. Fathers will be not only fathers to their children – they will be comrades and friends as well; mothers will be the same.

Young people always need someone to confide in. Whether it is a parent, pastor, counselor, or friend, there must be someone they trust with whom they can freely share their joys or struggles, and with whom they can talk openly about sex without shame or embarrassment.

Today's teenagers are simply presented with too many options. Our culture believes variety is the key to freedom; but far from it, it may be the key to confusion. Too few people are willing to warn teenagers of the painful emotional scars that follow on the heels of uncommitted sexual activity. There are even fewer who are able to point them to the hope of forgiveness after they have failed.

For this reason, trusted role models are especially needed. Children spend more time than ever on their own; across the social spectrum, latchkey kids are increasingly common. It is no accident that today's children have been dubbed by some experts as "Generation Alone," or that studies assign words like "abandoned," "alienated," and "alone" to describe them.

Lest we forget, purity, like impurity, is learned first and foremost by example (Titus 2:6–8). Children need to see that the love between their parents is indissoluble, and to know that certain looks, touches, and words of affection are appropriate only between a married man and woman. They need to see that physical intimacy belongs to marriage alone and that experimentation of any sort beforehand will only stain a later marriage. They certainly need to be spared the confusion and pain of broken relationships and sexual sin in or among adults around them.

That is why it is so important that the church has a central place in family life. Children must be able to see living examples of purity not only in their parents, but in everyone around them, whether married or single.

The best safeguard against sin is love.

Purity can never be fostered in a vacuum. Our children and youth need to gain a heart for Jesus and his cause of peace and social justice. When their hearts are filled with God and inspired for his cause, they will instinctively react against evil. When we lead them to recognize the needs of others, they will long to reach out in love. The idea that children have no social conscience, no feeling for the suffering, injustice, and guilt of our world is simply not true – this can only happen if they are brought up in an artificial environment that revolves around their own comfort and pleasure. When genuine children come face to face with the need of others, or when they see others reaching out to the needy, they will have an inner urge to extend their own love in practical ways.

The best safeguard against sin is always love. Love binds together all the virtues in perfect unity (Col. 3:14). Love is the message we need to bring to our children and youth, most importantly by demonstrating love in everything we ourselves say and do. So many young people today live for themselves and for their own interests. They work hard to get good grades, to excel in sports, to win the recognition earned by a scholarship – all of which is commendable. But how many of them care about their neighbors or the need of the world around them? We need to challenge and stretch our youth to interact with others, especially with others of different faiths and backgrounds.

Often parents try to protect their teenagers by anxiously shielding them from situations of impurity or violence, especially at high school or in college. Yet perhaps what they really need is the opposite: the opportunity to stand on their own feet and witness to what they themselves – not just their parents – believe.

Our children need to reach out and learn what others of their time are thinking and feeling. They need to relate to their peers and to the burning social, political, and economic issues of their day. They need to have a heart for the despair of those who have turned to drugs and alcohol, and for those who suffer from abusive relationships in the home. Without the ability to understand and relate to others outside their sphere, they will have no real connection to the world around them and will never be given the opportunity to test their own convictions.

We will never raise perfect children, but we firmly believe that it is possible to raise children who will respond to our guidance and discipline, in spite of the terrible corruption and darkness of our age (Prov. 22:6). As long as we are able to maintain a relationship of mutual respect and reverence, we will find the way forward with our children. It will cost a fight, sometimes a serious one, yet for the sake of a child's soul, a battle is always worthwhile. Naturally, our children may grow up to choose a path of life different from that which we would have chosen for them. But if we pray to Jesus for his guidance every day, we can be confident that he will lead us and them.

CHAPTER 13

For Those Considering Marriage

Train yourself to be godly. For physical training is of some value, but godliness has value for all things, holding promise for both the present life and the life to come...Don't let anyone look down on you because you are young, but set an example in speech, in life, in love, in faith, and in purity.

1 Timothy 4:8, 12

It is shocking how casually, and with what selfishness and naiveté, young men and women today plunge into relationships and even into marriage. Yet how should young people handle the natural attractions and friendships that develop between them? What is the godly approach? How can young men and women stay clear of the superficial eroticism of our time and find truly free and natural relationships? And how can they best prepare themselves for the responsibilities and demands of marriage?

Conventional dating cheapens the meaning of commitment.

We should rejoice when there are friendships between young men and women, and when there are opportunities for positive mutual exchanges in their daily lives. To have fear of what might go wrong among them is often unwarranted, and a sign of mistrust. Young people need opportunities to relate to each other in group settings where they can work, share, sing, or relax together. To pair off or form exclusive relationships is unhealthy and out of place: in the church, young men and women should get to know each other first as brothers and sisters. They must have the freedom to be seen together without being subjected to all sorts of gossip or speculation about their friendship. The pressure caused by such talk inhibits freedom. It skews and undermines everything that is good in a relationship.

It is typical of the immaturity of a young person to "fall in love" first with one and then with another, like a bee going from flower to flower. It is only natural to want to search for "the right one"; but the church cannot tolerate the continual forming and then dissolving of new relationships. The casual attitude of a young man or woman who flits from one boyfriend or girlfriend to the next is never right. It dulls the conscience and cheapens the meaning of commitment. The waves of emotional attraction that accompany every friendship between a boy and a girl are perfectly normal, but if they are not placed under Christ, they can leave wounds that may last a lifetime.

Because of this, my church rejects conventional dating. For the most part, dating in our society has become a game – a ritual of pairing off with a boyfriend or a girlfriend on the basis of physical and emotional attraction. It is built on a false understanding of friendship and often has little to do with genuine love or faithfulness. In many instances, dating is centered on an unhealthy preoccupation with personal "image." And when it involves physical or sexual intimacy, it can leave a conscience so heavily burdened that it takes years to heal.

Vanity and superficiality go hand in hand with conventional dating. So does flirting – drawing attention to oneself so as to sexually attract another person. Flirting demonstrates inner insecurity and unhappiness, and it is an insult to God.

In recent years more and more parents and churches are seeking alternatives to conventional dating. Some, for instance, are reviving the "old-fashioned" practice of courtship, which emphasizes mentoring, familial involvement, and character-enriching activities. Statistics also show that dating on college campuses is on the decline. Many college coeds now prefer to travel in "unpartnered packs," where group activity and personal accountability are stressed. These are indeed encouraging signs and they should encourage parents, pastors, and church leaders to become even more active and involved.

Mutual feelings are not sufficient for building a lasting relationship.

How should a young man or woman find the right partner? For a Christian the decisive factor should always be unity of heart and soul in the Spirit. Both partners must feel that their relationship leads them closer to Jesus, for his will alone can bring together two people who are meant for each other. Without Jesus and the special unity he gives between two people, a couple will very likely not survive the storms and struggles that are a part of every marriage, especially once they have children.

Even when a young couple is sure that they want to enter a more committed relationship, through engagement, for instance, they should test their love for a time to see whether it is merely the straw fire of romantic attraction, or whether there is something deeper. Again, physical and emotional attractions are natural, but they do not provide sufficient ground on which to marry or found a family, and can never be the deciding factors in making a commitment. A relationship based only on these is a shallow one, and eventually it will go to pieces. The real question should always be, "What does God want for our life and future together?" His will is the surest basis.

All of us have heard the saying, "It's what's on the inside that counts," but whether we truly believe it is another matter. Consciously or subconsciously, we have all judged other people on the basis of their physical appearance. In a culture where it is normal to hear someone say, "She's a very attractive young lady," or, "He's the good-looking one," and so on, it never hurts to think about the subtle message we are sending to those who are not described in this way.

The issue of judging people by their looks, or "lookism," is especially important for young couples considering marriage. A young woman may single out the most handsome guy around; or a young man, the prettiest girl in the bunch. But what about their relationship ten or twenty years down the road? Will they still love each other when he goes bald, when she gets wrinkles or gains weight?

Certainly physical attraction is a part of every relationship, but it can never be the basis for a life-long commitment of loyalty and love. As Isaiah put it, "All flesh is grass, and all its beauty is like the flower of the field. The grass withers, the flower fades..." (Isa. 40: 6–7).

It is not easy to see with the eyes of the heart, particularly when we are young. Yet we must ask God to give us this special sight. If we open our hearts to his wisdom, we will see beauty in every person we meet, and love each one as a fellow being created in the image of God.

I have known Rose ever since she was a young girl. As an adult, she met and fell in love with Tom. Tom is severely crippled by cerebral palsy and has spent his entire life in a wheelchair; all the same they married and now have two lovely children. To Rose, Tom is the most wonderful man in the world. Others may see only his disabilities, but Rose sees the beauty of his soul.

Victor and Hilda, a British-born couple from my community, lived into their nineties. Married in their twenties, they remained deeply in love to the end. Hilda was not beautiful in the worldly sense: by her seventies she was severely stooped, and a nervous twitch disfigured the right side of her face. Yet to Victor, she was always "my princess." Their love was grounded in something far deeper than appearance.

During the thirty years I have spent counseling young couples, many have shared their joys and struggles with me, but I am still touched every time a young person turns to me in trust. Not long ago a young woman wrote to my wife to tell her about her deepening friendship with a young man. Kate and Andy are both members of our church and participate in our youth group. They are not special people, but as their relationship continues to develop, a special gift is being given to them – a firm footing for their shared seeking. Kate writes:

> From the start this has been an intensely inner experience, and we have grown very close, especially through reading the Bible and praying together. I would say, though, that the biggest struggle has been to give up our romantic, emotional idea of love, because it really has so little place. Occasionally our conversation has gotten on the level of human attractions, and the effect of that is devastating because it undermines what we have experienced together on an inner, spiritual level...But when we keep God at the center, we find each other's hearts much more deeply.
>
> As we learn to know each other better, and know each other's day-to-day struggles and failings, we are also able to admonish and encourage each other. As a result, we both feel closer to God. More and more clearly I see how a relationship is not established once for all, but that it must be built on a daily basis – brick by brick – and with a faith that is constant. I am so thankful for the time Andy and I are sharing together, so that we can really establish a firm foundation. And I am also grateful that it has not all been smooth sailing, because nothing worthwhile comes without a struggle.

Andy and Kate's story is encouraging: even in our time it is still possible for young people to take their relationship to each other so seriously that they seek to find God above all else. In this connection we should remember Jesus' words, "Seek first the kingdom of God, and then everything will be added unto you."

If faith is the only firm foundation for Christian marriage, it follows that each partner must make a commitment to Christ and the church before making a commitment to each other. Here the importance of baptism cannot be emphasized enough. As a confession of repentance for sin and as the covenant of a clear conscience with God, baptism is one of the greatest gifts a person can experience. I would even say that without it, there is no secure foundation for a Christian marriage.

Of course, no one should be baptized for the sake of husband, wife, or children (Luke 14:26). Nor should the desire for baptism be mixed with feelings of desire for a potential marriage partner. If baptism is to have real meaning, it must be the seal of deep repentance, conversion, and faith.

A healthy relationship needs time and care.

Jesus says that we cannot serve two masters (Matt. 6:24). He teaches us that when we trust God alone, and trust him completely, he will provide for all our needs, including the need for a partner. "Seek first the kingdom of God and his righteousness, and all these things will be given to you as well" (Matt. 6:33). This advice is important not only for those who might be preoccupied with the question of marriage in an unhealthy way, but for all of us.

I would never expect a young person to give up marriage like the Apostle Paul did; the call to celibacy must be felt from within. But unless marriage is God's will (and this is often difficult to discern), every one of us should be willing to give it up (Phil. 3:8). When the light of Jesus breaks into our life, we will find strength to surrender to him so radically that everything will find its true proportion.

Contrary to the widely accepted belief that the healthiest relationship is the most private one, we feel that engagement and marriage are concerns of the whole church, not just of the individuals involved. Therefore, when young men and women in my church feel drawn to one another, I advise them to turn first to their parents, and then to a pastor. From this moment on their relationship is placed under the care of the church. Our youth do not regard this step as an imposition, nor do they feel they are being chaperoned. On the contrary, they are grateful for the possibility of guidance in an area where immaturity and impurity bring misery to many.

Naturally, this approach will only work in a congregation ruled by love and trust, and every couple must decide how it applies to their situation. For some, it may be hard to understand the purpose of seeking guidance. Others may shy away from the idea completely. Yet the simple lesson of opening up to people one trusts deserves serious attention.

Ray and his fiancée, Helen, met at our church afew years ago. Below, Ray shares their story:

> Saturday nights, when I wasn't working late at Armani Exchange, I'd go clubbing with a handful of friends. Or maybe head for Third Street in Santa Monica, or just drive down to the pier and hang out. The scene rarely changed. Only the girls. Nothing serious, never anything "going on" – just someone to split the tab on a few rounds or hit the dance floor with. Sometimes I'd meet someone I thought was special, someone I wanted to see more of. We'd trade numbers, and maybe arrange for the dinner-and-movie thing. It was all so harmless, so effortless.
>
> At least that's how I viewed it then, nearly three years ago, before I got to know Helen.
>
> Both of us grew up in the same church. We met as teenagers, but though we both had feelings for each other, we did not disclose these. After high school, we moved apart. She headed for college, and landed a teaching job; I left for

"the world." But after a six-month stint as a volunteer overseas, a couple semesters of college on the East Coast, and a year spent running around Southern California, the nagging sensation that my life was a farce finally cornered me. I had to admit what I had tried to deny for so long – that an intense emptiness and listlessness was masquerading behind my party-hard attitude. My lifestyle did nothing to satisfy my desire for wholeness. My encounters with others, particularly with women, were at best superficial. Often, they were damaging.

For the first time in my life I realized how much I needed the healing power that Christ alone can give. I knew I could not find this on my own, that I needed the support of others I could trust, so I returned home to my parents. Convinced that I wanted God to be the center of my life, I committed my life to him and to the members of my church.

By then I'd made my parents and my pastor aware of my feelings for Helen, and they advised me to let things develop naturally, in God's time: "If your relationship is God's will, it will happen, and no one will be able to stand in the way of it." But they encouraged me to go ahead and talk with her.

I did. It didn't take long for us to realize that something was happening between us. Neither of us would have dared call it love at the time – it was too new, too precious. But as weeks became months, we felt a deep connection growing between us. We spent time together, sometimes with each other's families, sometimes on our own. We would mull over issues of faith, read from the Bible, pray, or just sit quietly together. Later, when my job necessitated a move, we wrote to each other almost every day.

As our friendship deepened, our openness grew. But trust, we learned, takes time. At first, it was something of a revelation to realize that we both had shortcomings. We could hurt each other, and at times even betray the love taking shape between us. Yet whenever we became entrenched in our own

> narrowness, our parents and pastors were there to help guide us through.
>
> Of course, opening up to someone was sometimes painful, even embarrassing – especially when things weren't going smoothly. And the advice our parents or other church members would give didn't always sit well with us. But once we discovered the incredible value of having trusted people to confide in, we realized we were being granted an opportunity for our relationship to unfold within a supportive environment.
>
> Now, as our wedding nears, we are grateful for the help of others who have steered us toward Christ. Without them, Helen and I would most likely never have found each other's hearts. In our era, we know what a rare gift it is that our relationship has been able to deepen without the pressures caused by revolving around sex. And we know that no matter what our future brings, Christ will remain our guide.

Ray and Helen's story illustrates how vitally important it is for a couple to take plenty of time to get to know each other inwardly before making any commitment. When two people seek marriage, it is essential that they first strive to discover all there is of God in each other. There are plenty of wholesome activities a couple can find for this purpose: reading, hiking, visiting each other's families, or participating in a community service project together. Writing to each other is also a good way to become acquainted on a deeper level. In my experience, it is best if such correspondence starts out in a non-binding way – as if from a brother to his sister and vice versa. This is because emotional appeals about romantic love and belonging together, far from providing a foundation for the future, do the opposite: they obscure the discernment needed to discern whether or not a future commitment is really God's will.

My church encourages young couples not only to correspond by letter, but also to share these letters with either a parent or pastor. Such openness may seem extreme, but it allows for support and guidance, and is not resented. One can only wonder how many marriages might be saved if young couples everywhere had the humility to turn to their parents (or any other married couple they trust) for advice, even if not in this specific way.

Again, a healthy relationship cannot be rushed. Like a flower, it must be allowed to open in God's time, not forced in hopes of an early bloom. If a marriage is to last, it must be built on a carefully laid foundation.

What matters most, in the decision to marry, is God's will.

Honesty is fundamental to every true relationship. If a couple does not feel that they are growing closer to each other and to God, they must be open about it. Here the church, too, must care enough about its members to be honest with them – to help a couple discern if they are really meant for one another, and to consider whether their friendship is bearing good fruit. Even if no promise has been made, ending a relationship is painful. But better a painful end than the endless pain of a relationship that leads nowhere.

Only when two young people, independently of each other but with the input of their parents and minister, feel assured over a period of time that they really belong together for life are they ready to become engaged. Only when they feel in the depth of their hearts that their partner is the person meant for them, and that it is God alone who has led them together, are they truly ready to make a bond for life.

Once engaged, most couples want to participate fully in their love and express it actively in giving and receiving. Their hearts are set on making each other as happy and fulfilled as possible, and they feel ready to do anything to bring this about. All the more, such couples must realize that the powers of love are much greater than they themselves, and they must ask God daily for the strength to discipline themselves.

Long embraces, caressing, mouth-to-mouth kissing, and anything else that might lead to sexual arousal should be avoided. The desire for physical closeness between two is natural, but instead of revolving around this desire, an engaged couple should focus on getting to know each other more intimately on an inner level and nurturing each other's love to Jesus and the church.

When two people are getting to know each other, sexual involvement inhibits the development of a well-founded relationship. As soon as sex is on stage, it steals the show. Sexual excitement is progressive in its nature: once you begin you are never satisfied in going back. When two people intentionally arouse each other, they are engaging in a form of foreplay. Whether they acknowledge it or not, they are preparing themselves emotionally and physically for intercourse. They are left with only two choices: to go all the way, or to stop short and experience the emotional frustration of being aroused and not satisfied. The desires kindled within them cannot be appeased without sinning. "Going halfway" is therefore harmful, because it interferes with building lasting intimacy.

A marriage that starts with a conscience burdened by unconfessed sin is a marriage without a stable foundation, and it can be set right only through confession and repentance. The health of a marriage depends on the ground in which it grows. If it is sown in the soil of purity and faith, it will bear good fruit and have God's blessing.

Try to grasp the spirit, not the letter, of what I have written. Seek to understand each other's inmost heart, and turn to Christ in absolute trust to seek his answer to every question. He will never fail to lead you clearly.

CHAPTER 14

The Service of Singleness

The disciples said to him, "If that is the situation between a husband and wife, it is better not to marry." To this Jesus replied, "That is something which not everyone can accept, but only those for whom God has appointed it. For while some are incapable of marriage because they were born so, or were made so by men, there are others who have themselves renounced marriage for the sake of the kingdom of heaven. Let those accept it who can."

Matthew 19:10–12

The gift of unity, whether with other people or with God, does not depend in any way on marriage. In fact, the New Testament teaches that a deeper dedication to Christ may be found by giving up marriage for the sake of the kingdom of God. Those who renounce everything for Jesus, including the gift of marriage, are given a great promise by him: he will be especially near to them at his return (Rev. 14:1–5). Whether such people find themselves without a life partner because of abandonment, death, or lack of opportunity, they can find a much greater calling than marriage if they are able to accept their singleness in the depth of their hearts. They can dedicate their lives in a special way to undivided service for God's kingdom.

To live fully is to live for Christ.

Every man and every woman on earth who desires to follow Christ must be completely transformed by him. This challenge takes on a deeper meaning for those who are single (for whatever reason) and who carry their singleness for Christ's sake. Such a person will find a special relationship to him.

A life lived for Christ is life in its fullest sense (John 10:10). We must never forget this; it is our deepest calling. If we truly love Christ the Bridegroom with undivided hearts, we will be immersed in him just as we are immersed in water at baptism. If we live in Christ, our love for him will guide our love to our brothers and sisters and to all those around us.

The story of Francis of Assisi and his friendship with Clare shows in a wonderful way the significance of brotherly and sisterly love – even when it does not lead to marriage. When all of Francis's brothers and friends deserted him, he went to Clare. In her he had a friend he could rely on. Even after his death she remained loyal to him and continued to carry out his mission, despite opposition. Here was a relationship that had nothing to do with marriage but was still genuinely intimate – a friendship of true purity and unity in God.

There will always be women and men like Clare and Francis who remain unmarried for the sake of Christ. Yet we must recognize that the gift of a relationship such as theirs is not given to everyone. In struggling for purity, most single people are no different from married people. Singleness is no safeguard against impurity – in every heart, purity requires constant watchfulness, a daily fight against the flesh, and a firm attitude against sin.

If we allow him,
Jesus can fill every void.

The Scriptures never promise us the removal of temptation. But we do have the assurance that it need not overcome us (1 Cor. 10:13). If we prove ourselves in patience and faithfulness, God will help us. This is not to say that it is possible to keep pure by the strength of our own will. Yet by the power of the Holy Spirit, and through the help of caring friends and family members, it is possible to find freedom and victory (Gal. 6:1–2).

For those who do not find a partner in marriage but feel no special calling to remain single for the sake of Jesus, there is a danger of bitterness. If a deep yearning for marriage remains unfulfilled, especially over a long period of time, it can harden the heart. Then only God's grace can protect the soul and enable it to let go – to give up marriage and still find peace.

Cynthia, an unmarried woman in her mid-forties, offers her insights on how to avoid an empty life and find lasting fulfillment:

> "Me, single for the rest of my life?" Many of us must face this reality. Why? – because we have chosen to commit our lives to God first. He needs tools that are unattached to family to serve him. Does this mean less fulfillment, stunted growth, withdrawal from full involvement in life? Not if one

can embrace, instead of rebel against, God's plan for one's life. In fact, a dedicated life of service awaits those who sacrifice or renounce marriage in order to keep themselves completely at God's disposal.

Think of single people like the writer Amy Carmichael, who traveled to India as a young missionary, not knowing what kind of service God wanted of her. She soon had a growing orphanage of children rescued from virtual slavery in the clutches of the Hindu temple priests. Or think of Mother Teresa, who founded an order of sisters to look after the poorest of the poor in Calcutta. Her order has spread all over the world. Or think of Paul and others of the apostles who, because they were single, were able to travel ceaselessly to spread the Gospel.

Of course you don't have to be a missionary, nun, or apostle to find fulfillment in a life of singleness. I could have felt bitterness and frustration at not being married, but instead I have found plenty of opportunities to serve others on a daily basis right where I have been placed.

Almost weekly I visit inmates at the local jail. During my last visit, the women in the jail were eager for bible study, so we read the story of the Good Samaritan and talked about its everyday applications. After a discussion of who could or couldn't sing, we all joined in singing spirituals and hymns like "Precious Lord" and "Amazing Grace."

Needless to say, not every evening is satisfying in this way. Loneliness can be a real part in the life of any single person. It may tempt one to self-pity, but like any temptation, it can be refused. In her book *Passion and Purity*, Elisabeth Elliot advises: "Accept your loneliness. It is one stage, and only one stage, on a journey that brings you to God. It will not always last. Offer up your loneliness to God, as the little boy offered to Jesus his five loaves and two fishes. God can transform it for the good of others. Above all, do something for somebody else!"

> Here is the clue: service rendered to others. Teaching, nursing, counseling, or visiting prisoners in jail – any of such activities can lead to a fulfilled life. For there are many hurting people in the world who need an extra touch of love, and those of us who are single are uniquely free to take up the task of being there for them.

The process of letting go to one's own desires is never easy, and it may at times weigh very heavily on a person. But when single people are able to surrender their own hopes and dreams completely, Jesus will fill the void that might otherwise burden them. They will remember how he ended his life on the cross, and they will find joy in bearing singleness as their sacrifice for him. Those who continually long for marriage, despite the fact that God has not given it to them, can never attain this joy. Marriage is a great gift, but to belong completely and undividedly to Christ is a greater gift.

Ultimately, we have to be willing to be used by God as he wills and find contentment in whatever circumstances we find ourselves (Phil. 4:11–13). We should never think that God does not love us. Such a thought is of the devil.

Naturally, no matter how dedicated a single person is, he or she will still experience moments, days, even weeks, of sadness and struggle. The knowledge that marriage and children are beyond reach will always bring pangs of longing and a sense of loss. But rather than dwell on these things, it is better (even if harder) to look to God and to turn to one's brothers and sisters in the church. Bonhoeffer writes:

> Pain is a holy angel who shows us treasures that would otherwise remain forever hidden; through him men and women have become greater than through all the joys of the world.

> It must be so and I tell myself this in my present situation over and over again. The pain of suffering and of longing, which can often be felt even physically, must be there, and we cannot and need not talk it away. But it needs to be overcome every time, and thus there is an even holier angel than the one of pain; that is, the one of joy in God.[24]

Singleness can be accepted as a burden – or as a higher calling.

Single men and women must not fall into the trap of estranging themselves from life and love in bitterness. They must not stifle what is best in themselves or give themselves over to dreams or to desires that cannot be satisfied. They must not let self-circling fantasies block the unfolding of all that God has given them. If they are able to accept their singleness as a gift or a special calling, they will let none of their energy or love go unused. Their longings will be fulfilled in giving: in a stream of love that moves away from themselves, and toward Christ and the church. As Paul says:

> An unmarried man is concerned about the Lord's affairs – how he can please the Lord. But a married man is concerned about the affairs of this world – how he can please his wife – and his interests are divided. An unmarried woman or virgin is concerned about the Lord's affairs: her aim is to be devoted to the Lord in both body and spirit. But a married woman is concerned about the affairs of this world – how she can please her husband. I am saying this for your own good, not to restrict you, but that you may live in a right way in undivided devotion to the Lord (1 Cor. 7:32–35).

Earlier in the same letter, Paul refers to another blessing of singleness: the lack of care and worry over spouse and children, especially in times of hardship. "Those who marry will have pain and grief in this bodily life, and my aim is to spare you" (1 Cor. 7:28).

Widows, like the unmarried, are also able to serve the church and the needy at times when a married person could not. Paul says, "A woman who is really widowed and left without anybody can give herself up to God in hope and consecrate all her days and nights to petitions and meetings for prayer" (1 Tim. 5:5). In the early church in Jerusalem, widows were appointed to serve the poor or entrusted with other responsibilities. "In even the smallest church community the overseer had to be a friend to the poor, and there had to be at least one widow responsible to see to it, day and night, that no sick or needy person was neglected."[25]

How sad it is that today it is very often the widows – and other single women and men – who are themselves neglected and lonely! May the church always be ready to meet the needs of such people (1 Cor. 12:26). Especially with the collapse of the family, we must find new ways to show single members extra love and care and to involve them in the lives of their families or fellowships. This does not mean pressing them to find a spouse and then pitying them if they don't – that will only add to their pain. It means welcoming their gifts and services in the church, providing them with meaningful tasks, and drawing them into the inner life of the church so that they may find fulfillment.

No matter our state,
all of us are called to love.

Those of us who are married should recognize that our happiness is a gift – something to be shared and passed on. We should want to reach out to those who struggle with feelings of loneliness. Most important, all of us, whether married or single, should remember that true fulfillment and joy is found in serving one another in the spirit of community. We are called to a love that gives unconditionally – not to the grasping love of a cozy marriage nor to the indulging love of isolated self-pity.

As Christians, we know that true love is found in its most perfect form in Jesus. Many of us have been touched by Jesus, or been called and used by him. But that is not enough. Each of us must ask God to let us experience him personally – in the very depths of our hearts. Our eyes must be fixed on him and him alone so that we can see him as he really is, and not grow weary and lose heart (Heb. 12:2–3).

The span of life is short, and as Paul warns us, the world in its present form is passing away (1 Cor. 7:29–31). What we need most in our time is Christ, but not only as a guide or an image before our eyes. He must become a living force in our daily lives. He said, "I came on earth to kindle a fire. How I wish it were already burning!" (Luke 12:49)

Where is Christ most clearly revealed as he was and still is? We must seek for him with our brothers and sisters. We must ask that he is revealed today and every day among us. More than that, we must ask for the courage to witness to him before others just as he is, with tenderness, meekness, and humility, but also in truth, clarity, and sharpness. We must not add or take away anything. That is the essence of single-heartedness, and the service of singleness.

The Spirit of Our Age

CHAPTER 15

With or Without God

Be imitators of God, therefore, and live a life of love, just as Christ loved us and gave himself up for us...Among you there must not be even a hint of sexual immorality, or of any kind of impurity, or of greed, because these are improper for God's holy people. Nor should there be obscenity, foolish talk, or coarse joking...Let no one deceive you with empty words, for because of such things God's wrath comes on those who are disobedient.

Ephesians 5:1–6

Throughout Scripture the covenant of God with his people and the unity of Christ with his church is compared to the union of marriage. In our culture, however, marriage – the very thing we should honor and celebrate most as love – has been attacked, dragged into the dirt, and destroyed by the spirits of impurity and irreverence.

For many people today, love is a delusion.

The desecration of love is one of the greatest tragedies of our time. Increasingly, love is understood as nothing more than selfish desire, and the satisfaction of this desire is seen as fulfillment. People talk about sexual liberation but remain trapped in bondage to their sexual desires; they talk about true love but live in self-absorbed estrangement. Our age is a loveless age: relationships and hearts are broken everywhere, millions of human lives are discarded almost before they have begun, thousands of children are abused or abandoned, and fear and mistrust abound even in supposedly healthy marriages. Love has been reduced to base sex. Because of this, it is nothing more than a delusion for many – short-lived intimacy followed by gnawing emptiness and anguish.

How can we rediscover the real meaning of love? So many things in the world today take away our belief in lasting and unconditional love. So much of what has to do with "love" these days really has to do with the excitement and passion of lust. We live in a sex-obsessed, sex-crazed society, and everything reeks of it – advertising, literature, fashion, and entertainment. Marriage has been the first casualty: its significance has become so distorted that its true meaning has been lost.

Of course, no honest person can lay the blame for all of this at the door of the media or of some vague force in society. Certainly, the media has confused thousands of people and left them hardened. But it is we – each one of us – whose souls are burdened by the sin of our own lust, whose marriages have fallen apart, whose children have gone astray. We cannot ignore our own misdeeds; we must take responsibility for our own actions, for every instance where we have accepted the spirit of impurity and let evil into our own hearts. We have mocked and twisted the image of God and separated ourselves from our creator. We must learn to listen again to the deepest cries of our hearts, and repent and turn back to God.

Thirty years have passed since the beginning of the sexual revolution, and its devastating aftermath should be obvious to anyone: widespread promiscuity; rising rates of teen pregnancy and suicide; tens of millions of abortions; the spread of sexually transmitted diseases; the erosion of the family and home life; and the rise of a violent new generation. "We have sown the wind, and reap the whirlwind" (Hos. 8:7).

Our time grossly overestimates the importance of sex. Whether on bookstands, in convenience stores, or at supermarket counters, its significance is exaggerated in a thoroughly unhealthy way. Love between man and woman is no longer regarded as sacred or noble; it has become a commodity seen only in an animal sense, as an uncontrollable impulse that must be satisfied.

As a tool of the sexual revolution, modern sex education more than anything else is responsible for all this. Sex education was supposed to bring us freedom, enlightened attitudes, responsibility, and safety. Isn't it obvious by now that it has been a failure? Haven't we seen by now that knowledge is no safeguard, and that sex education as taught in most schools has only increased sexual activity?

True education for the sexual life instills reverence.

Most parents have very little, if any, idea of what their children are taught in sex education classes. Sex education has never been a simple presentation of biological facts. In many curricula students are graphically taught (sometimes by way of films) about various sexual practices, including masturbation, and about "safe" sex. In others, sexual perversions are openly and explicitly discussed and presented as normal ways of finding sexual "fulfillment." In some school districts an appreciation and understanding for the homosexual lifestyle is encouraged: it is, our children are told, a perfectly acceptable alternative to heterosexual marriage. Some schools even have students pair off to discuss topics such as foreplay and orgasm. Antibiotics and abortion are presented as positive safety nets in case contraception and safe sex practices fail. Abstinence, if not entirely ignored, is mentioned only in passing. As William Bennett, former Secretary of Education, writes:

> There is a coarseness, a callousness, a cynicism, a banality, and a vulgarity to our time. There are too many signs of a civilization gone rotten. And the worst of it has to do with our children: we live in a culture that at times seems almost dedicated to the corruption of the young, to ensuring the loss of their innocence before their time.[26]

Sex education is little more than "safe" sex training. Initially, it was instituted as an attempt to bank the fires of teenage sexuality; instead, it has only fanned the flames.[27] Most people seem to take it for granted that teenagers will and should express themselves sexually. Our era is one of millions of abortions, of countless unwed mothers on public support, and of epidemic sexually transmitted diseases. Clearly, the idea that accurate knowledge fosters responsible behavior is nothing less than a grand myth.

In general, much of what is taught today in the name of sex education is a horror, and as Christians we must protest against it. It is often little more than the formalized training of irreverence, impurity, and rebellion against the plan of God.

True education for the sexual life takes place best between parent and child in an environment of reverence and trust. To educate anyone about sex through anonymous images and impersonal information will only awaken the sexual impulse of a child prematurely and, in his mind, separate sex from love and commitment.

Obviously we should not be afraid to talk freely with our own children about sexual matters, especially as they approach adolescence. Otherwise they will learn about these things first from their peers, and rarely in a reverent atmosphere. All the same, there is a danger in giving a child too many biological facts about sex. Often, a factual approach to sex robs it of its divine mystery.

To the Christian parent, sex education means guiding the sexual conscience of his or her children to sense their own dignity and the dignity of others. It means helping them to understand that selfish pleasure, whether it "hurts" anybody else or not, is contrary to love (Gal. 5:13). It means teaching them that, separated from God, sexual intercourse or any other sexual activity burdens the conscience and undermines honest relationships. It means opening their eyes to see the deep emptiness that leads people – and could lead them too – into sexual sin.

A child can acquire a healthy attitude to his body and to sex quite naturally, simply by being taught that his body, as the temple of the Spirit, is holy, and that any defilement of it is sin. I will never forget the deep impression it made on me as a young teen when my father took me for a walk with him and told me about the struggle for a pure life and the importance of keeping myself pure for the woman I might find and marry some day. He said to me, "If you are able to live a pure life now, it will be easier for the rest of your life. But if you give in now to personal impurity, it will become harder and harder to withstand temptation, even once you marry."

Parents who want to protect their children from impurity should remember that the discipline of work – whether through chores, exercise, or through other activities – is one of the best safeguards. Children who have been taught to stick to a task and see it through will be better equipped to deal with sexual temptations than children who have been pampered and catered to.

Any misuse of sex cuts us off from our true selves and from each other.

Young people underestimate the power of the demonic forces they allow into their lives when they give in to impurity. Take masturbation, for example. As children grow into young men and women, their sexual desire increases, and often their most immediate urge is to seek sexual gratification through masturbation. Increasingly, parents, educators, and ministers of our day claim that masturbation is healthy and natural; many see it as just another form of stress release. And the sexual activity it often leads to, even among children who have barely reached puberty, is considered by some to be normal.

Why are we parents and educators so afraid to speak the truth – to warn our children not only of the dangers of promiscuity but also of masturbation? (Prov. 5:1 ff.) Aren't both illnesses of the soul? Don't both desecrate and betray the image of God, and undermine the marriage bond? Masturbation can never bring true satisfaction. It is a solitary act. It is self-stimulation, self-gratification, self-abuse – it closes us within a dream world and separates us from genuine relationships. When it becomes habitual (which it often does), it aggravates isolation and loneliness, and it intensifies feelings of futility and frustration. At its worst, as a breach in the bond of unity and love for which sex is created, it is comparable to adultery. I have counseled many young people who are enslaved by masturbation: they earnestly desire to be freed from their habit, but they fall into it again and again.

A person who struggles with masturbation is often too ashamed to talk about it with anyone. Yet it is important to realize that because shameful acts work in secrecy, their power can only be broken when they are brought to light. Certainly sharing one's burdens and inner feelings with a mentor or pastor can be painful, but this is the only recourse for anyone who wants to become truly free.

People may struggle with masturbation right to the end of their lives. I have counseled men in their eighties who still have not found freedom from it. The question arises whether there is anything one can do to be rid of this curse. My advice to those enslaved to masturbation is to seek strength through prayer. You will not conquer your addiction by will power alone. Before you go to bed at night, turn your thoughts to God and read something of an inner, spiritual nature. Even then the temptation to masturbate can arise. When that happens, find something to take your mind off it – get out of bed and take a walk, or do some household chore. Often a simple activity provides the best means to overcome these strong temptations.

Frequently enslavement to masturbation is connected to another form of bondage: pornography. Very few people will admit an addiction to pornography, but the fact that it is a steadily growing billion-dollar industry shows how widespread it is, also among "Christians."

Many people claim that pornography should not be criminalized because it is "victimless." Yet anything that encourages impurity, even in the form of solitary sexual arousal, is a crime because it degrades the human body, which was created in God's image as a temple of the soul (1 Cor. 6:19). The so-called lines typically drawn between pornography, masturbation, one-night stands, and prostitution are actually an illusion. All of them are means used to attain sexual satisfaction without the "burden" of commitment. All reduce the mystery of sex to a technique for satisfying lust. And all of them are shameful – the secrecy of those who indulge in them betrays that fact more clearly than anything else (Rom. 13:12–13).

Prayer and confession can free us from the burden of impurity.

No one can free himself from impurity or any other sin in his own strength. Freedom comes through the attitude of inner poverty, through continually turning to God. The struggle against temptation is in everyone and will always be there, but through prayer and confession, sin can be overcome.

Whenever we let down our guard in the struggle for purity – whenever we allow passion and lust to overcome us – we are in danger of throwing ourselves completely away. Then we will not be able to drive away the evil spirits we have allowed to enter, and the intervention of Christ himself will be needed to bring freedom. Without this, there will be only deepening hopelessness and despair.

In the most extreme instances the desperation brought on by a secret life of impurity ends in suicide. This can only be described as a rebellion against God, a statement that says, "I'm beyond hope – my problems are too big even for God to handle." Suicide denies that God's grace is greater than our weakness. If we find ourselves in the abyss of despair, the only answer is to seek God and ask for his compassion and mercy. Even when we find ourselves at the end of our rope, God wants to give us new hope and courage, no matter how deeply we feel we have betrayed him. God is always ready to forgive every sin (1 John 1:9); we only need to be humble enough to ask him. When someone is tempted by thoughts of suicide, the most important thing we can do is to show him love – to remind him that each of us was created by and for God, and that each of us has a purpose to fulfill.

To turn from sin and to realize that we are created for God is always a revelation and a joy. If we faithfully face God in our lifetime here on earth, we will recognize the magnitude of our wonderful task, the task of receiving his love and sharing it with others. There is no calling more wonderful.

CHAPTER 16

Shameful Even to Mention?

Live as children of light (for the fruit of the light consists in all goodness, righteousness, and truth) and find out what pleases the Lord. Have nothing to do with the fruitless deeds of darkness, but rather expose them. For it is shameful even to mention what the disobedient do in secret.

Ephesians 5:8–12

In June 1995, a panel of the Church of England recommended that the phrase "living in sin" be abandoned and that unmarried couples, heterosexual and homosexual alike, be "given encouragement and support" in their lifestyles and more readily welcomed into Anglican congregations. Suggesting that "loving homosexual relations and acts" are intrinsically no less valuable than heterosexual ones, the panel proposed that love should be allowed to be expressed "in a variety of relationships."[28] Although such a statement is hardly surprising in today's world, it is shocking to hear it from an established church, and to know that other church denominations have asserted similar ideas.

**We must love the sinner,
but we must also speak out against sin.**

Recently I served on a parent-teachers' committee at a local high school and was able to observe just how powerful the movement to accept homosexuality has become – how it has crept into almost every aspect of public life. The school district's Health and Safety Advisory Committee was so afraid of alienating gays and lesbians that it was hesitant even to define "family," let alone take a position on so-called family values. Finally, it settled on defining "family" as "two people with a commitment."

Many politicians and an increasing number of clergy are afraid to say anything against such a definition for fear of losing voter support or their jobs. Very few dare to stand in opposition and say, "Enough!" But by refusing to define marriage as a covenant between one man and one woman, they not only call into question the entire institution of the family but flatly deny God's order for creation. They are sending our children the message that anything is okay, and that life-long commitment to one partner of the opposite sex is merely one of many options.

To some readers it may seem that I am advocating hatred toward homosexuals – "gay bashing." Let me assure you that I am not. Every one of us is a sinner and falls short every day, and there is no biblical basis for making homosexuality a worse sin than any other. To make fun of homosexuality or to judge a practicing homosexual any more harshly than another person who has sinned, or to look on him or her with an attitude of condemnation, is a sin: we know from the gospels that no sexual sin is so terrible that it cannot be forgiven or healed (Eph. 2:3–5). Yet we also know that Jesus hates sin, even though he loves the sinner and wants to redeem him.

To affirm homosexuality is to deny God's creative intent.

Homosexual conduct is a sin. It is "against nature," against God's creative design, and it is a form of self-worship and idolatry (Rom. 1:26). As a sexual act between two people of the same gender it is the "very grievous" sin of Sodom and Gomorrah (Gen. 19:1–29).

In Leviticus 18:22–23, God calls homosexual intercourse an abomination: "Do not lie with a man as one lies with a woman; that is detestable." And in Leviticus 20:13 we read, "The penalty for homosexual acts is death to both parties. They have brought it upon themselves." Let those who discount such prohibitions and warnings by explaining that we are now "no longer under the law, but under grace" then explain why incest, adultery, bestiality, and human sacrifice are not to be ignored. All of these are condemned in the very next sentences: "Do not have sexual relations with an animal and defile yourself with it. A woman must not present herself to an animal to have sexual relations with it; that is a perversion."

The New Testament also condemns homosexuality. In Romans 1:26–28 Paul writes:

> Their women have exchanged natural intercourse for unnatural, and their men in turn, giving up natural relations with women, burn with lust for one another; males behave indecently with males and are paid in their persons the fitting wage of such perversion.

And in 1 Cor. 6:9–10 Paul writes:

> Do you not know that the wicked will not inherit the kingdom of God? Do not be deceived; neither the sexually immoral nor idolaters nor adulterers nor male prostitutes nor homosexual offenders...will inherit the kingdom of God.

Many people reinterpret these Scriptures as condemning only homosexual rape, promiscuity, and lustful or "unnatural" homosexual behavior by heterosexuals. They claim that what the Bible condemns is *offensive* homosexual (and heterosexual) behavior. But isn't it clear that when Paul speaks of "homosexual offenders" he is speaking of the offense of homosexuality itself? If only "offensive" kinds of homosexual acts were evil, then what about the rest of what Paul mentions in the same passage: adultery, idolatry, and so forth?

What could be clearer than Paul's words in Romans, where he calls homosexuality "sinful desire, sexual impurity" and says that it is "degrading and shameful"? Or his unmistakably sharp words against giving oneself over "to depravity"? (Rom. 1:24–28) Homosexual acts are always perverse, for they always distort God's will for creation. They simply cannot be defended in any way by Scripture. And this is just as true when they take place in a "loving" lifelong relationship. Adulterous heterosexual affairs may also be felt to be loving and may be long-lasting, but that doesn't make them right.

It is typical today to hear people complain about the injustice of holding homosexuals responsible for an orientation or even a way of life that they themselves did not necessarily choose. But this is only an excuse for sin. Whether or not homosexuals are responsible for their sexual orientation has no relevance as to the rightness or wrongness of their behavior. To explain behavior is one thing. To justify it is altogether different.[29]

Whatever its origin or kind, sexual temptation can be overcome.

The sexual urges of a homosexual can be acute, but so can those of anyone else. All of us are "naturally" predisposed to do what we should not do. But if we believe in God, we must also believe that he can give us the grace to overcome whatever struggles we may have to bear: "My grace is sufficient for you, for my power is made perfect in weakness" (2 Cor. 12:9–10).

In speaking out against homosexuality, we must always remember that even though Scripture condemns homosexual behavior, it never gives us license to condemn the people who engage in it. As Christians we certainly cannot condone the denial of any person's basic human rights, for whatever reason. It is all too easy to forget that the Bible has much more to say about pride, greed, resentment, and self-righteousness than about homosexuality. Nevertheless, we will always resist the agenda of those who try to redefine homosexuality as an "alternative lifestyle" – especially as it affects the legalization of same-sex marriages – as well as efforts to compel religious groups to accept practicing homosexuals as members and even ministers (1 Cor. 5:11).

It is also important to consider the difference between homosexual tendency or "orientation" and an active homosexual lifestyle. Whereas homosexual orientation can arise by means of psychological influences, social environment, and perhaps (according to some scientists) even genetic makeup, an active homosexual lifestyle is a matter of choice. To argue that our culture, family, or genes make us powerless to choose for or against sin is to deny the concept of free will.

Even as an orientation, homosexuality is an especially deep-rooted condition, and those who struggle with it deserve compassion and help. Therefore we always need to be ready to receive the homosexual man or woman into our fellowship and stand with him or her – in patience and love, though also with the clarity that refuses to tolerate continued sexual sinning. Above all, we need to remind those burdened with same-sex attraction of God's original plan for creation, and help them see that neither man nor woman is truly complete without the other.

I have counseled many people who have struggled with homosexual temptations. Sometimes a person's situation seems hopeless, but in my experience, even someone who has been ingrained in the "gay lifestyle" for a long time *can* be helped. Whether a struggling homosexual acts on his temptations or not, one thing remains the same: if he turns single-mindedly to Jesus, he can be helped and freed; if he is divided in the depth of his heart, even the most valiant efforts to resist temptation will cramp him in an inner way. Even a perverse glance shows that a person is not decided – and Jesus calls this "adultery" in the heart. Lasting freedom can be found only in decisiveness.

It is all the more important, therefore, that people who are not burdened by homosexuality try to understand the tremendous inner need of those who are. Their misplaced sexual desire often stems from an intense yearning for a genuinely loving connection with others. Many homosexuals have never known unconditional, accepting love from those of their own gender. In fatherless homes across our country, a void exists that is capable of inducing homosexual feelings in children. And in our culture, driven as it is by competition and the will to dominate, it is easy for some people to feel left out; they may turn to homosexuality as a result.

I have known Howard and his wife, Ann, ever since they joined our church two decades ago, yet it was not until recently that I fully understood the depth of Howard's struggle. Abused as a child by his uncle, neglected by his workaholic father, and ridiculed by his peers for his lack of athletic ability, Howard grew up feeling misunderstood and out of place. He craved attention: from his father, other men, and boys his own age. By the time he was in his mid teens, he was homosexually active. While Howard does not blame his upbringing for choices he made later in life, his story should warn every parent of what can happen when children grow up without the support of a caring family.

But Howard's story is more than a warning. It bears witness to Christ's power to overcome darkness; to the importance of repentance; to the healing force of forgiveness; and to the joy that every one of us can know. He writes:

> When I was sixteen, I began to mess around with other boys. It wasn't long before I allowed older men to "experiment" with me. These sexual experiences excited me, but they left me feeling very guilty. I was not able to open up to anyone about what I was going through. I even lied to my father when he confronted me directly and asked if I had such feelings.
>
> By the time I turned twenty-one, I had done virtually every homosexual act possible. Nothing satisfied me. My encounters with other men were empty; I preferred to look at pictures and create my own fantasies. I never tried to come to terms with my attraction to men, excusing it as something I "couldn't help." Even when my insurance paid for psychotherapy

because of work-related stress and anxiety, I did not tell the psychiatrist anything personal. I was convinced: there was no point talking to anyone; no one would understand me, and it wasn't possible for me to change, anyway.

I married the first woman I had a sexual relationship with. Ann loved me and accepted what she knew of me. We talked about our personal feelings, but not until we'd been married over two years did I work up the courage to share my secret with her. Naturally, Ann responded with stunned surprise. She could not understand how it was possible. I told her about my childhood and about the thoughts and desires that burdened me. I made it clear to her that I wanted nothing to do with these things, and she accepted this and seemed to have hope that I could change. Even though I fell into casual encounters with other men on several more occasions, she continually forgave me.

Many homosexuals were "coming out of the closet" at that time, revealing their lifestyle to family and friends and trying to find acceptance. I dreaded this, because I was sure I would not be accepted. Actually, at heart I did not want acceptance; I wanted help to overcome my problem. Finally I told my story to a lay pastor whom I trusted. He helped me find the strength to declare my stand against homosexuality before a small group of people I knew and felt close to. They were at first shocked, but then also very supportive, knowing that they too had struggles. This was a beginning of my path to recovery. But only the beginning.

Later my wife and I joined the Bruderhof, a Christian community movement, sensing that we had arrived at a place where true healing could be found. To a degree this was true, but sometimes when I felt low and depressed, I would still give in to lustful thoughts and looks, which on several occasions nearly led me back into my old ways. Clearly I could never overcome my problems in my own strength. All the same, I kidded myself into believing I could, and convinced my wife I was doing okay. In the meantime, I was blocking out Jesus' words about the lustful look. My conscience became duller and duller. My heart grew harder and harder.

Ann continued to trust me, and God gave us two sons. Yet in spite of these blessings, I sunk deeper and deeper. Then one day a friend discovered me looking at pornography. Though at first I tried to lie my way out, I finally found the courage to admit my sin, both before my wife and the brothers and sisters within my community. "Everyone" now knew, and I waited to be "run out of town." But while no one condoned my behavior, I did not feel condemned. Men who I thought would be totally disgusted with me suddenly looked me squarely in the eyes with true, brotherly love. My hard heart began to melt...

My wife and I separated for several weeks so that I could find my true bearings again. During this time Ann stood faithfully by her commitment to the church and to me. She told me later, "When we married, I had no idea what we might face in the future. We promised to remain faithful – come hell or high water – to God, to the church, and to each other. We had no idea what we were promising, but I know this is what protected us. This is what led us together again."

Ann was right, of course. It was only through God's grace that I was able to recognize how badly I needed to come completely clean, to open up my heart wider than I ever had before, and to set straight every single wrong act or ingrained attitude from the past. I saw how my own selfishness lay at the root of my problem. Bit by bit, I felt my bondage to darkness breaking.

As my repentance deepened, my heart grew lighter, my mind freer. Finally, I moved back in with my wife and children. Now we are closer as a family than we ever have been. And the curse I have lived with all my life has been transformed into a deep joy. Christ has given me the gift of a clear conscience – there is no greater gift. It gives me courage to

> face anything that might come in the future. I know I will be tempted for the rest of my life, but I also know that there is always a way through. I can receive help beyond my own strength.

True freedom is possible for every man and woman, and it is up to us to believe this (Gal. 5:1).[30] Howard and Ann's story should remind us not to pretend that victory is easy. It may not be. For every person who is granted healing, there are dozens more who have to struggle with temptations for years, some for the rest of their lives. Yet is it any different for the rest of us? There cannot be many Christians who have not longed and prayed, seemingly without result, for deliverance from some besetting sin. But we should never doubt that since each of us is created in God's image, there is hope for healing and restoration for each of us (Heb. 9:14). Ultimately, Christ will free us if we give ourselves to him.

CHAPTER 17

The Hidden War

You brought me out of the womb; you made me trust in you even at my mother's breast. From birth I was cast upon you; from my mother's womb you have been my God. Do not be far from me, for trouble is near and there is no one to help.

Psalm 22:9–11

Almost seventy years ago, in response to the idea of "modern" family planning, Eberhard Arnold wrote, "In our families we hope for as many children as God gives. We praise God's creative power and welcome large families as one of his great gifts."[31]

What would he say now, in an era where contraception is standard practice and millions of unborn children are legally murdered every year? Where is our joy in children, and in family life? Our thankfulness for God's gifts? Where is our reverence for life and our compassion for those who are least able to defend themselves? Jesus is very clear that no one can enter the kingdom unless he or she becomes like a child.

Sex without regard for the gift of life is wrong.

The spirit of our age is diametrically opposed not only to the childlike spirit but even to children themselves. It is a spirit of death, and it can be seen everywhere in modern society: in the rise of murder and suicide rates, in the widespread domestic violence, in abortion, the death penalty, and euthanasia. Our culture seems bound on going the way of death, of taking into its own hands what is God's domain. And it is not only the State that is at fault.

How many churches sanction the murder of unborn children under the guise of supporting women's rights? The sexual "liberation" of our society has sowed tremendous destruction. It is a false liberation built on the selfish pursuit of satisfaction and pleasure. It ignores discipline, responsibility, and the real freedom that these can bring. In the words of Stanley Hauerwas, it mirrors "a profound lack of confidence that we have anything worthy to pass on to a new generation...We are willing our deaths."[32]

It is simply a fact that the vast majority of people today have no qualms of conscience when the life of a tiny being is prevented or destroyed. Children, once considered the greatest blessing God can give, are now considered only in terms of their cost: they are a "burden" and a "threat" to the freedom and happiness of the individual.

In a true marriage, there is a close connection between married love and new life (Mal. 2:15). When husband and wife become one flesh, it should always be with the reverent recognition that through it new life may be formed. In this way the marriage act becomes an expression of creative love, a covenant that serves life. But how many couples today view sex in this way? For most, the pill has made intercourse a casual act, divorced from responsibility and supposedly free of consequence.

As Christians, we must be willing to speak out against the contraceptive mentality that has infected our society. Too many couples today have simply bought into the popular mindset of sexual indulgence and family planning on demand, throwing to the wind the virtues of self-control and trust. Sex for its own sake, even in marriage, not only cheapens the marriage act but erodes the foundation of self-giving love necessary for raising children. To engage in sexual pleasure as an end in itself, without regard for the gift of life, is wrong. It means closing the door to children, and thus despising both the gift and the Giver (Job 1:21). As Mother Teresa once said:

> In destroying the power of giving life, through contraception, a husband or wife is doing something to self. This turns the attention to self, and so it destroys the gift of love in him or her. In loving, the husband and wife must turn the attention to each other, as happens in natural family planning, and not to self, as happens in contraception.

Contraception undermines the fulfillment and fruition of two who are one flesh, and because of this we should feel revulsion toward the attitude that consistently seeks to avoid the responsibility of bearing children.

None of this is to suggest that we are to bring children into the world irresponsibly or at the risk of the mother's health and well-being. The size of one's family and the spacing of children is a matter of tremendous responsibility. It is something for each couple to consider before God, with prayer and reverence. Having children too closely together can place an especially difficult burden on the mother. This is an area where a husband has to show loving respect and understanding for his wife. Again, it is vital that a couple turn together to God and place their uncertainties and fears before him in faith (Matt. 7:7–8). If we are open to God's leading, I am confident that he will show us the way.

To abort any child is to mock God.

The contraceptive mentality is but one of the manifestations of the spirit of death that makes new life so unwelcome in so many homes. Everywhere in society today there is a hidden war going on, a war against life. So many little souls are desecrated. And of those who are not prevented by contraception from entering the world, how many are callously destroyed by abortion!

The prevalence of abortion in our society is so great that it makes Herod's slaughter of the Innocents tame in comparison. Abortion is murder – there are no exceptions. If there were, the message of the gospels would be inconsistent and meaningless. Even the Old Testament makes it clear that God hates the shedding of innocent blood (Prov. 6:16–17). Abortion destroys life and mocks God, in whose image every unborn baby is created.

In the Old Testament there are numerous passages that speak of God's active presence in every human life, even while it is still being formed in the womb. In Genesis 4:1 after Eve conceives and gives birth to Cain, she says, "With the help of the Lord, I have brought a man into being." She does not say, "With the help of Adam," but "with the Lord."

In Psalm 139 we read:

> For you created my inmost being; you knit me together in my mother's womb. I praise you because I am fearfully and wonderfully made; your works are wonderful, I know that full well. My frame was not hidden from you when I was made in the secret place. When I was woven together in the depths of the earth, your eyes saw my unformed body. All the days ordained for me were written in your book before one of them came to be (Ps. 139:13–16).

Job exclaims: "Did not he who made me in the womb make them? Did not the same One form us both within our mother's womb?" (Job 31:15; 10:8–12)

And God said to the prophet Jeremiah, "I knew you before you were formed within your mother's womb; before you were born I sanctified you and appointed you as my spokesman to the world" (Jer. 1:5).

We also read in the New Testament that the unborn are called by God before birth (Gal. 1:15) and that their unique gifts are prophesied while still in the mother's womb. Perhaps one of the most wonderful passages about an unborn child is found in Luke:

> When Elizabeth heard Mary's greeting, the child leaped in her womb. And Elizabeth was filled with the Holy Spirit and exclaimed with a loud cry, "Blessed are you among women, and blessed is the fruit of your womb. And why has this happened to me, that the mother of my Lord comes to me? For as soon as I heard the sound of your greeting, the child in my womb leaped for joy" (Luke 1:41–44).

Here an unborn child, John the Baptist, the forerunner of Jesus, leaped in Elizabeth's womb in acknowledgment of Jesus, who had been conceived only a week or two before. Two unborn children: one capable of responding to the

Holy Spirit, and the other – none other than Christ himself – conceived by the Holy Spirit (Matt. 1:20–21).

Clearly, the idea that a new little life comes into being through something merely physical or biological is a complete falsity. It is God who acts in bringing forth life from the womb (Ps. 71:6). Abortion always destroys this act.

This is why the early church universally rejected abortion, and called it infanticide. *The Didache*, the earliest instruction (100 C.E.) for new Christian converts, leaves no doubt about that: "You shall not slay a child by abortion." And Clement of Alexandria even writes that those who participate in an abortion "wholly lose their own humanity along with the fetus."[33]

Where is the clarity of the church today? Even among so-called Christians, the war of cruelty and death being waged against the innocent unborn children has become a matter of fact, its ghastly horrors and brutal techniques hidden by the mask of medicine and law or even "justified" by every thinkable circumstance.

Who are we to judge whether a life is desirable or not?

I know it is unpopular to say that abortion is murder. I know that people will say I am removed from reality – that even certain Christian theologians make at least some allowances for abortion. Yet I believe God never does. His law is the law of love. It stands forever, regardless of changing times and changing circumstances: "Thou shalt not kill."

Human life is sacred from conception to death. If we really believe this, we will never be able to accept abortion on any grounds; even the most persuasive arguments about "quality of life" or severe physical deformity or mental retardation will not sway us. Who are we to decide whether or not a little soul should reach the light of day? In God's plan the physically and mentally hindered can be used for God's glory (John 9:1–3). "Who has made man's mouth? Who makes him dumb, or deaf, or seeing, or blind? Is it not I, the Lord?" (Exod. 4:11)

How can we dare to judge who is desirable and who is not? The crimes of the Third Reich – where "good" Nordic babies were bred in special nurseries, while retarded babies, children, and adults were sent to gas chambers – should be warning enough. As Dietrich Bonhoeffer writes, "Any distinction between life that is worth living and life that is not worth living must sooner or later destroy life itself."[34]

Even when the life of a pregnant mother is in danger, abortion is never the answer. In God's eyes, the life of the unborn child and mother are equally sacred. To do evil "so that good may come" is to take God's sovereignty and wisdom into one's own hands (Rom. 3:5–8). In agonizing situations like this, a couple should turn to the elders of their church:

> Is anyone among you suffering? He should keep on praying about it. And those who have reason to be thankful should continually be singing praises to the Lord. Is anyone sick? He should call for the elders of the church and they should pray over him and pour a little oil upon him, calling on the Lord to heal him. And their prayer, if offered in faith, will heal him, for the Lord will make him well; and if his sickness was caused by some sin, the Lord will forgive him (James 5:13–15).

There is great power and protection in the prayer of a united church and in the faith that God's will can be done for both the life of a mother and her unborn child. In the end – and I say this with trembling – that is what matters.

We must offer alternatives, not moral condemnation.

As Christians, we cannot simply demand an end to abortion without offering a positive alternative. Eberhard Arnold writes:

> Moral philosophers may demand that the sexual life be purified by insisting on purity before and in marriage. But even the best of them are insincere and unjust unless they clearly state the actual basis for such high demands. Even the destruction of incipient life...remains unassailable when people do not believe in the kingdom of God. The supposedly high culture of our day will continue to practice this massacre as long as social disorder and injustice last. Abortion cannot be combated as long as private and public life are allowed to remain as they are.
>
> If we want to fight acquisitiveness and the deceit and injustice of social distinctions, we must fight them through practical means by demonstrating that a different way of life is not only feasible, but actually exists. Otherwise we can demand neither purity in marriage nor an end to abortion; we cannot wish even the finest families to be blessed with the many children intended by God's creative powers.[35]

Here the church has failed miserably. There are so many teenage mothers who are confronted by this question daily, yet receive no inner guidance, no emotional or economic support. Many feel they have no other choice than abortion: they have been the victim of sexual abuse; or they fear an angry boyfriend; or their parents have pressured them, saying that if they have the baby they can't come home.

In speaking with groups of women who have had abortions, author Frederica Mathewes-Green discovered a near unanimous consensus as to why women have abortions: in nearly every case it is because of relationships. Women do not want abortions, she writes. They want support and hope.

> I have found that a woman is most likely to choose abortion in order to please or protect the people that she cares about. Often she discovers too late that there is another person to whom she has obligations: her own unborn child. The grief that follows abortion springs from the conviction that, in a crisis, this relationship was fatally betrayed.
>
> Supporting women with unplanned pregnancies means continuing what pregnancy-care centers have been doing all along: providing housing, medical care, clothing, counseling, and so forth. But we should also be paying attention to becoming a steadfast friend, the most important help we can give, and to doing whatever we can to repair relationships in the family circle.[36]

In speaking out against abortion, therefore, we must not forget that few other sins cause more heartache or anguish of soul. Very few women today are offered viable alternatives, and almost none of them are pointed to God, who alone can answer their need. A woman who has had an abortion suffers great torment of conscience, and her isolation and endless pain can be healed only at the cross – only by finding Christ. Christians need to feel the immeasurable pain that so many women bear in their hearts for their lost children. Who of us can cast the first stone? (John 8:7) Woe to us if we ever become cold toward a woman who has had an abortion!

God loves the unborn child in a very special way. After all, he sent us his only son, Jesus, to earth in the form of a baby, through the womb of a mother. As Mother Teresa points out, even if a mother turns against her unborn child, God will not forget him. He has carved each baby in the palm of his hand and has a plan for each life, not only on earth but for eternity. To those who are desperate enough to hinder God's plan, we say with Mother Teresa, "Please don't kill the child. I want the child. Please give the baby to me."

CHAPTER 18

What about Divorce and Remarriage?

Everyone who divorces his wife and marries another commits adultery, and he who marries a woman divorced from her husband commits adultery.

Luke 16:18

The question of divorce and remarriage is possibly the toughest issue that faces the Christian church in our time. It is harder and harder to find couples who take seriously the words, "What God has joined together, let no one put asunder" – couples who believe that marriage means faithfulness between one man and one woman until death parts them (Matt. 19:6).

A marriage bond may break, but it can never be dissolved.

The majority of Christians today believe that divorce and remarriage are morally and biblically permissible. They argue that though God hates divorce, he allows it as a concession to our sinful condition. Because of our hardness of heart, they explain, marriages can "die" or dissolve. In other words, God recognizes our frailty and accepts the fact that in a fallen world the ideal cannot always be realized. Through God's forgiveness, one can always start again, even if in a new marriage.

But what about the bond that is promised between two and made – whether knowingly or unknowingly – before God? Does God's forgiveness ever mean we can deny it? Does he ever allow unfaithfulness? Just as the unity of the church is eternal and unchangeable, so true marriage reflects this unity and is indissoluble. As the early Christians, I believe that as long as both partners are living, there can be no remarriage after divorce. What God has joined together in the unity of the Spirit is joined together until death parts a couple. Unfaithfulness, whether by one or by both partners, cannot change this. No Christian has the freedom to marry someone else as long as his or her spouse is still living. The bond of unity is at stake.

Jesus is clear that it was because of hard-heartedness that Moses, under the law, allowed divorce (Matt. 19:8). However, among his disciples – those born of the Spirit – hard-heartedness is no longer a valid excuse. Moses said, "Whoever divorces his wife, let him give her a certificate of divorce." But Jesus said, "Everyone who divorces his wife, except on the ground of unchastity, makes her an adulteress; and whoever marries a divorced woman commits adultery" (Matt. 5:31–32). The disciples understood this decisive word of Jesus clearly: "If this is the situation between a husband and wife, it is better not to marry" (Matt. 19:10). Moses gave allowance to divorce out of sheer necessity, but this hardly changes the fact that from the beginning marriage was meant to be indissoluble. A marriage cannot be dissolved (even if it is broken), neither by the husband who abandons his adulterous wife, nor by the wife who abandons her adulterous husband. God's order cannot be abolished that easily or lightly.[37]

Paul writes with the same clarity to the Corinthians:

> Now to the married I command, yet not I but the Lord: a wife is not to depart from her husband. But even if she does depart, let her remain unmarried or be reconciled to her husband. And a husband is not to divorce his wife (1 Cor. 7:10–11).

He also writes, "A woman is bound to her husband as long as he lives. But if her husband dies, she is free to marry anyone she wishes, as long as he belongs to the Lord" (1 Cor. 7:39). And in Romans he says, "and if she marries another man while her husband is still alive, she is an adulteress" (Rom. 7:3).

Because adultery is a betrayal of the mysterious union between one man and one woman who become one flesh, it is one of the worst forms of deceit. Adultery must always be squarely confronted by the church, and the adulterer must be called to repentance and disciplined (1 Cor. 5:1–5).

The answer to a broken bond is faithfulness and love.

Even if Jesus allows divorce for reasons of fornication or adultery, it should never be the inevitable result or an excuse to remarry. Jesus' love reconciles and forgives. Those who seek a divorce will always be left with the stain of bitterness on their conscience. No matter how much emotional pain an unfaithful partner causes, a wounded spouse must be willing to forgive. Only when we forgive can we ever hope to receive the forgiveness of God for ourselves (Matt. 6:14–15). Faithful love, to our spouse but especially to Christ, is the only answer to a broken bond.

Kent and Amy, who now minister together in the same church in Colorado, were once divorced from each other. Their situation was as desperate as a marriage could get. Yet because they kept the door open to Christ they found each other again. Kent shares:

> From day one, our marriage had gigantic problems, and we began a three-year downward spiral into utter confusion. I thought marriage was just a matter of hanging out with my wife and doing fun things together. I had no idea what hard work it involved. Eventually I became a shell of a person and even despised life at times. I tried doing all the "spiritual" things I was supposed to do: reading the Bible, praying, and talking with others. But it all seemed so futile. Amy and I came from completely opposite backgrounds and, hard as we tried, we couldn't communicate.
>
> The pain grew so great that we decided to separate and to begin divorce proceedings. This was absolutely against my church upbringing, but I felt hopelessly trapped and had to get out. Yet even after we decided to divorce, the pain remained constant. I became so emotionally drained that there were mornings when I couldn't even button my shirt. Unable to cope, I stepped down from my pastoral position. All during this time Amy was utterly devastated. I knew she wanted things to be different, but it was all too overwhelming for me. Despite our commitments to Christ and to each other, we were both completely lost.
>
> To deal with my pain, I resorted to work. I knew that I would get into big time trouble if I allowed myself to become idle or to become involved in another relationship. So I worked and worked – and worked. Subconsciously I think both Amy and I tried to trust God, but daily I swore to myself that I would never get back together with her. Every time we tried to talk things out, we ended up fighting. It was hopeless.

I came to a point where I couldn't even turn to God anymore. Everything became so pointless, so dead: What did it all matter? Why was I working so hard anyway? Who was I trying to fool? Why try to do God's will if nothing good ever came from it?

But late one night, as I left work, the moon and the stars caught my eye. Something grabbed my heart, and I felt anew God's majesty and mercy. In a matter of seconds I was reduced to tears. In all my pain and despair I began to feel, perhaps for the first time, both my true need and God's unconditional love. Although I had become unfaithful to my promises to God and to my wife, God assured me that he was still faithful to me and that he had not given up on me. That night was a real turning point. By the miracle of God's grace, something inside me began to change.

I wish I could say that there were a lot of miraculous events that brought Amy and me back together again. But there weren't. We found each other through a lot of hard work. There was no instant reunion; it took two years. We had to do a lot of talking and a lot of forgiving. But as we shared, a lot of the pain and the emotion that was there before disappeared. In the end, it was God who rescued us. It was he who helped us keep the door open to him and to each other – in spite of ourselves. It was he who spared us the lie that one's problems are best solved by getting involved with some other, more suitable person.

Our marriage still goes through rough patches. Perhaps it always will. We are still very different from each other. And if I dwell too much on my weaknesses or Amy's, it is tempting to try and find a way out. But God's faithfulness binds us together and preserves our love for each other. And it is this faithfulness that keeps me focused and committed.

Of course, not every marital struggle ends as happily as Kent and Amy's. In my church it has happened several times that a married partner becomes unfaithful, divorces his or her spouse, and remarries. Almost every time, the partner left behind has decided to remain in our church, faithful to his or her vows of membership and of marriage. Though this is naturally a painful choice – and doubly so when there are children involved – it is part of the cost of discipleship. If we believe in God, he will give us the strength to hold fast.

When I marry a couple, I always ask them the following question, which was formulated by my grandfather, a dissident pastor in Nazi Germany.

> My brother, will you never follow your wife – and my sister, will you never follow your husband – in what is wrong? If one of you should turn away from the way of Jesus and want to forsake his church, will you always place faith in our Master, Jesus of Nazareth, and unity in his Holy Spirit above your marriage, also when confronted by government authorities? I ask you this in the knowledge that a marriage is built on sand unless it is built on the rock of faith, faith in Jesus, the Christ.

As pertinent today as in its original context, there is deep wisdom in this question. In a sense, it is simply a reminder of the choice set before each of us who claim to be disciples: are we ready to follow Jesus at all costs? Didn't he himself warn us, "Whoever comes to me and does not let go of father and mother, wife and children, brothers and sisters, yes, and even life itself, cannot be my disciple"? (Luke 14:26)

If a couple takes this warning seriously, it may bring about separation, but the sanctity of their marriage bond will actually be protected. The issue here is not only marriage as such, but the deeper bond of unity between two people united in Christ and his Holy Spirit (1 Cor. 7:15–16).

Whenever a man or woman remains loyal to his or her partner – no matter how unfaithful that partner may be – it is a witness to this unity. The eternal faithfulness of God and his church can always engender new commitment and hope. I have seen more than once how the faithfulness of a believing partner can lead an unbelieving partner back to Jesus, back to the church, and back to a strong marriage.

Ann and her husband, Howard (whose story I shared in chapter 16), are an example of this. Even when Howard fell back into sin, Ann never wavered from her commitment to Christ and the church. Yet though she refused to go along with Howard's deceit, she did not judge him. Instead, she quietly led him in the struggle for repentance and a fresh start. Largely as a result of Ann's steadfastness, both their marriage and Howard's faith were restored.

True faithfulness is not merely the absence of adultery.

Though God hates divorce, he will also judge every unloving or dead marriage, and this should be a warning to each of us. How many of us have been cold-hearted or loveless to our spouses at one time or another? How many thousands of couples, rather than loving each other, merely coexist? True faithfulness is not simply the absence of adultery. It must be a commitment of heart and soul. Whenever husband and wife lack commitment to each other, live parallel lives, or become estranged, separation and divorce lurk around the corner.

It is the task of every church to fight the spirit of adultery wherever it raises its head. Here I am not only speaking of adultery as a physical act; in a sense, anything inside a marriage that weakens love, unity, and purity, or hinders the spirit of mutual reverence, is adultery, because it feeds the spirit of adultery. That is why God speaks of the unfaithfulness of the people of Israel as adultery (Mal. 2:10–16).

In the Old Testament, the prophets use faithfulness in marriage as a picture of God's commitment to Israel, his chosen people – his bride (Hos. 3:1). In a similar way, the Apostle Paul compares marriage to the relationship of unity between Christ, the bridegroom, and his church, the bride. Only in the spirit of these biblical images can we clearly consider the question of divorce and remarriage.

When a church does nothing to nurture the marriages of its own members, how can it claim innocence when these marriages fall apart? When it shies away from testifying that "what God has joined together, no one should put asunder," how can it expect its married members to remain committed for life?

In considering these questions, there are two pitfalls we must avoid. First, we can never agree to divorce; second, we must never treat those who suffer its need and pain with legalism or rigidity. In rejecting divorce, we cannot reject the divorced person, even if remarried. We must always remember that though Jesus speaks very sharply against sin, he never lacks compassion. But because he longs to bring every sinner to redemption and healing, he requires repentance for every sin. This is also true for every broken marriage.

Clearly, we must never judge. At the same time, however, we must be faithful to Christ above everything else. We must embrace his whole truth – not just those parts of it that seem to fit our needs (Matt. 23:23–24). That is why my church will not marry divorced members (at least as long as a former spouse is still living) and why we cannot accept divorced and remarried couples as members, as long as they continue to live as husband and wife. Remarriage compounds the sin of divorce and precludes the possibility of reconciliation with one's first partner. We stand for lifelong fidelity in marriage. No other stand is consistent with real love and truthfulness.

The significance of the marriage commitment needs to be rediscovered. We are only beginning to confront the harm that divorce does to our children. For children, let alone for adults, divorce is something you don't just "get over." Recent studies show that the majority of children whose parents divorce are worried, underachieving, and self-deprecating. Even ten years after their parents break up, they still suffer from such emotional problems as fear and depression, and display antisocial behavior.

Stepfamilies do not provide the answer. The original family structure cannot be restored, however hard one tries to simulate it. In fact, children living with stepparents often show more insecurity than children in single-parent homes.[38] A generation of children is growing up without parents who act as true role models – and many children simply do not have real parents at all. As well-intentioned as many of today's young people are, where can they find support when it is time to marry and start a family?

With God, all things are possible.

Naturally, if divorce is to be avoided, the church must offer its members guidance and practical support long before their marriages collapse (Heb. 10:24; 12:15). Even if there are only slight indications that a marriage is at risk, it is best to be honest and open about it. Once a couple drifts too far apart, it may take space as well as time for them to find each other's hearts again. In a situation like this, as in one where a partner has become abusive, temporary separation may be necessary. Especially when this is the case, the church must find concrete ways to help both partners – first in seeking repentance and then in finding the mutual trust and forgiveness necessary to restore the marriage.

It is sad that in today's society, faithfulness is so rare that it has come to be seen as a "heroic" virtue. Shouldn't it be taken for granted as the bedrock of our faith? (Gal. 5:22) As followers of Christ, shouldn't each of us be willing to hold firm through thick and thin, until death, to Christ, to his church, and to our husband or wife? Only with this resolve can we hope to remain faithful to our marriage vows.

The way of discipleship is a narrow way, but through the cross anyone who hears the words of Jesus can put them into practice (Matt. 5:24). If Jesus' teaching on divorce and remarriage is hard, it is only because so many in our day no longer believe in the power of repentance and forgiveness. It is because we no longer believe that what God joins together can, by his grace, be held together; and that, as Jesus says, "With God, all things are possible."

Nothing should be too hard for us when it is a requirement of the gospel (Matt. 11:28–30). If we look at Jesus' teaching on divorce and remarriage in this faith, we will see that it is one of great promise, hope, and strength. It is a teaching whose righteousness is much greater than that of the moralists and philosophers. It is the righteousness of the kingdom, and it is based on the reality of resurrection and new life.

CHAPTER 19

Therefore Let Us Keep Watch

The night is nearly over; the day is almost here. So let us put aside the deeds of darkness and put on the armor of light. Let us behave decently, as in the daytime, not in orgies and drunkenness, not in sexual immorality and debauchery, not in dissension and jealousy. Rather, clothe yourselves with the Lord Jesus Christ, and do not think about how to gratify the desires of the sinful nature.

Romans 13:12–14

Despite the shamelessness and promiscuity of our time, we believe that purity and faithful love are still possible today. Even if the established churches have neglected to proclaim the message that sexual happiness is possible within the commitment of marriage alone, we are still certain of its truth. There is no question that many people today have a deep longing for purity and faithfulness. But longing is not enough. Only when we are willing to follow and obey the leading of the Holy Spirit, cost what it may, can we experience its great blessings in our daily lives. Do we believe deeply enough in the power of the Spirit? Are we willing to let God transform our hearts so completely that he turns our lives upside down? (Rom. 12:2)

The struggle for purity demands daily resolve.

All of us know temptation, and all of us have given in to temptation. All of us have failed at one time or another – in our relationships at work and at home, in our marriages, and in our personal lives. The sooner we face that, the better. Yet we can take comfort, even if we struggle with ups and downs, and even if our moments of victory are followed by moments of doubt. Even Jesus was tempted, and he was tempted in every way we are (Heb. 4:15). With his help we can find the purity that protects us from every temptation. James says, "Blessed is the one who stands firm in temptation" (James 1:12). What matters here is the deepest will of our heart – the will that speaks within us whenever we come before God in prayer.

As we struggle to be faithful, it is of greatest importance that our entire will is decided for purity. A divided heart will never be able to stand (James 1:6–7). But willpower alone cannot bring about single-mindedness. If we work ourselves into an inner frenzy, even if we manage to keep our head above water, we will soon tire out and sink. Only if we surrender to Jesus can the power of his grace fill us and give us new strength and resolve.

In combating the spirit of our age, we must fight not only against the obvious sins of fornication, deceit, murder, and so on, but also against apathy and fear. Hardly anyone will say that he is against faithfulness and love, or opposed to justice and peace, but how many of us are ready to fight for these things in word and in deed? The spirit of our time has dulled us with such a deathly complacency that we are usually content to look the other way. But if we do not speak out against the evil of our time through the actions of our lives, then we are just as guilty as those who sin deliberately. We must all change, and we must start by confronting the indifference in our own lives.

Less than half a century ago, most people recognized premarital sex, divorce, homosexual activity, and the like as morally wrong. But today these things are regarded as acceptable lifestyle alternatives. Sadly, many churches take this stance as well. Now bestiality (sex with animals), pedophilia (sex with children), and sadomasochism are gaining support as means of "sexual expression." Only a few decades ago, transsexualism – the practice of undergoing a surgical male-to-female or female-to-male sex change – was unheard of. Today this godless practice is gathering momentum across the western world. The enormous cost of these surgeries alone is a crime against humanity when one thinks of the widespread hunger and poverty in the Third World and in our own American ghettos.

Frightening as all these trends are, parents should not be afraid to warn their children about the horror of these perversions. For even though Jesus says that all sin can be forgiven, my experience in counseling has shown me that those who engage in such practices can permanently wound their souls.

What must God think of the shamelessness of our time? In *The Brothers Karamazov*, Dostoevsky reminds us that "if God does not exist, everything is permissible." Are we not now seeing "everything?" When will we stop to consider the horrifying spirit of rebellion behind our sinfulness and remember God's warnings about his wrath on sinners in the end time? Let us remember the words of Paul: "You shall reap what you sow." Let us ask God for the mercy of his judgment before it is too late. Let us ask him to shake our deadened consciences, to cleanse us, and to bring us new life.

We desperately need more people like John the Baptist today. But where are they? Where are the "voices in the wilderness" crying out for repentance, conversion, faith, and a new life? John's message was simple: "Repent, for the kingdom of God is at hand!" He was not afraid to confront anyone, including the leaders of his day. He even confronted King Herod on his adulterous marriage, saying, "It is not lawful for you to have her" (Matt. 14:3–4). Perhaps most significant, though, he called to account the devout and religious, the "good" people: "You brood of vipers! Who has warned you to flee from the wrath to come? Therefore bear fruits of repentance" (Matt. 3:7–8).

In the fight for God's kingdom, good deeds are not enough.

In the Gospel of Matthew, Jesus says to his disciples, "The harvest is plentiful but the workers are few" (Matt. 9:37). How much truer is this today! So many people long for the freedom of Christ but remain chained to their sins. So few people dare to stick out their necks. The task is great.

Most of us have good intentions; we earnestly desire to do good deeds. But that is not enough. We dare not forget that the fight for God's kingdom is not just against human nature: we are dealing with something far more powerful, with powers and principalities (Eph. 6:12), and with the destructive, demonic spirit that John calls the "beast from the abyss" (Rev. 11:7).

This beast holds sway over every country and every government, and its mark is to be found everywhere in our day: in the disappearance of lasting friendship and community, in the oppression of the poor, and in the exploitation of women and children. It is to be seen in the wholesale murder of the unborn and the execution of the imprisoned. Most of all, it is to be seen in the lonely desperation of so many millions of people.

We are living in the end time. It is the last hour (1 John 2:18). We must be on the watch continually if we are not to fall under judgment in the last hour of temptation. We need to seek the inner strength and courage to speak up for God and his cause, even if no one seems willing to hear us.

Jesus' parable of the ten virgins should be a warning and a challenge to all of us. Jesus is not speaking here about the lost world on the one hand and the church on the other: all ten of the women in the story are virgins, and all of them are preparing to meet him. He is challenging the church:

> The kingdom of heaven will be like ten virgins who took their lamps and went out to meet the bridegroom. Five of them were foolish and five were wise. The foolish ones took their lamps but did not take any oil with them. The wise, however, took oil in jars along with their lamps. The bridegroom was a long time in coming, and they all became drowsy and fell asleep.
>
> At midnight the cry rang out, "Here's the bridegroom! Come out to meet him!" Then all the virgins woke up and trimmed their lamps. The foolish ones said to the wise, "Give us some of your oil; our lamps are going out."
>
> "No," they replied, "there may not be enough for both us and you. Instead, go to those who sell oil and buy some for yourselves." But while they were on their way to buy the oil,

> the bridegroom arrived. The virgins who were ready went in with him to the wedding banquet. And the door was shut.
>
> Later the others also came. "Sir! Sir!" they said, "Open the door for us!" But he replied, "I tell you the truth, I don't even know you."
>
> Therefore keep watch, because you do not know the day or the hour (Matt. 25:1–13).

Are we willing to demonstrate that a new way exists?

We cannot merely run from the challenge of sin. Instead, we must live in active protest against everything that opposes God. We must openly fight everything that cheapens or destroys life, everything that leads to separation and division. But we must also recognize that protest alone, which often leads to violence, is not sufficient. To simply renounce the world, reject marriage, or refuse all pleasure would be fruitless.

We must demonstrate that a new way exists and show the world a new reality, the reality of God's righteousness and holiness, which is opposed to the spirit of this world. We must show with our lives that men and women can live lives of purity, peace, unity, and love wherever they dedicate their energies to working for the common good; and not only by creating spiritual community, but by building up a practical life of sharing. Above all, we must witness to the power of love. Each of us can give our lives to others in the service of love. That is God's will for humankind (John 13:34–35).

In order to demonstrate God's will, the church must first take concrete steps toward forming a genuine sexual counter-culture. This demands committed effort. Chastity programs are not enough. Marriages and families will continue to splinter unless the church forms a *life together* on totally different terms. Christian families, along with their ministers, need to pledge to live their personal and social lives in contrast to the ways of the world. Unless we relate to each other on a different plane from the world's, we have little to protest or to say. If we are going to be serious about pursuing purity in this world, then we will need to hold each other, as brothers and sisters, accountable. This applies to everyday life: the way we dress and look, what we allow into our homes, how we and our children relate to the opposite sex.

The visible witness of such a community will do far more to convince our society than a million pamphlets on abstinence. Christian ideals can be explained, but moral principles are never enough. Only when the world sees living proof that a Christ-centered sexual life is possible – one where true freedom goes hand in hand with reverence and responsibility – will people welcome such values and norms.

However, wherever God's will is consistently lived out, it will be misunderstood and seen as provocation (1 Pet. 4:4). Two thousand years have not made our present world any more tolerant of Jesus' message than the world of his time. Those who are unwilling to accept his way will always be resentful and even vindictive toward those who witness to it, and a clash is inevitable (John 15:18–20). But if we who claim to follow Christ are afraid to live out his commands because we fear persecution, who will do it? And if it is not the task of the church to bring the darkness of the world into the light of Christ, whose is it?

Our hope is in God's coming kingdom, which is the wedding feast of the Lamb. Let us wait faithfully for that day. Every word we say, everything we do, should be inspired and influenced by our expectation. Every relationship, every marriage, should be a symbol of it. Jesus, the bridegroom, expects a bride prepared and waiting for him. But when he comes, will we be ready? Will we be "a radiant church, without stain or wrinkle"? (Eph. 5:27) Or will we be full of excuses? (Luke 14:15–24)

We must never be afraid of the ridicule and slander our witness will bring on us. What grips us and drives us should be God's future – the wonderful future of his kingdom – not the present "realities" of human society. It is God who holds the final hour of history in his hands, and each day of our lives should be a preparation for that hour.

From a Reader

You've finished reading *Sex, God, and Marriage*. Now what? The answer depends on how seriously you take up the challenge to be part of a "sexual counter-culture," one in which wholesome relationships have a chance to thrive. This doesn't have to be theory. And as the following letter from a reader illustrates, there is no need for anyone to have to struggle alone. Together, we can spread the message that a pure life – a life of true freedom and joy – can belong to each one of us, provided we are willing to work for it.

Dear Mr. Arnold,

While on vacation, I discovered *Sex, God, and Marriage* in a bookstore. I had never heard of you or your community before, but the book's title caught my attention, and seeing Mother Teresa's name on the cover convinced me to buy it. (She has been an extremely strong influence on my life.) The next thing I knew, I was reading it nonstop and calling each of my friends to tell them, "This book will change your life."

I know that books affect people in different ways, depending on where they happen to be in their life journey. I was born and brought up in a strong Catholic family, and for my entire life I have been able to witness my parents' stable, peaceful, Christ-centered marriage. They have made life so happy, even innocent, for us children. From the time we were old enough to understand, my parents taught us to reject the whole culture of abortion and birth control and to stick to the truth about these life issues. They tried their best to teach us to live for Christ alone.

But by the time I happened across *Sex, God, and Marriage*, I had reached a point where I once again needed some clear-cut, well-defined answers. Your book saved my life – saved my virginity, saved my interior convictions, saved my dignity.

I decided once and for all that struggling to uphold chastity was not going to be such a problem for me anymore, that if I really loved Jesus I would prove it to Him through a commitment to purity. I know we will always struggle with sexual desires; I know that temptation absolutely surrounds those who are striving to become saints. But I just needed to see these truths much more clearly: I don't *have* to get into sexual predicaments. Things *can* be stopped before they start. I've always known this, but your book confirmed for me once and for all that this was the truth.

And so I have been distributing *Sex, God, and Marriage* to all my friends. The letters and calls of response have been tremendous: "My life is different now." Or, "This has helped my marriage." Even, "I'm sending a copy straight away to my Mom and to my in-laws." One girl showed it to her friend, who read it from cover to cover and said, "I have to go to confession." She hadn't been for nine years. I have shared this book with all kinds of friends – Catholics, Baptists, Episcopalians – and the power it has to bind the Christian community together is amazing.

As for me, I know now, more strongly than ever, that everything I do must be for Jesus. Reading *Sex, God, and Marriage* showed me that my relationship with my boyfriend needed to end. It made me sad to leave him, but I think I showed him a greater act of love by not sticking around than by leading him, or have him lead me, into a sinful situation. Your book has also increased my desire to want to read the Bible. I now have more reverence and awe for the miracle of life and sex than I ever had before. With deepest appreciation, I thank you for this gift of rejuvenation you have given to me and to so many others.

In Christ,
M. B.

Notes

[1]For a summary of current data on the effects of non-marital sex, read *Why Marriage Matters: Reasons to Believe in Marriage in Postmodern Society*, by Glenn T. Stanton (Colorado Springs, CO: Pinon Press, 1997).

[2]Johann Christoph and Christoph Friedrich Blumhardt, *Now is Eternity* (Rifton, NY: Plough, 1976), 13.

[3]Thomas Merton, *New Seeds of Contemplation* (New York: New Directions, 1972), 180.

[4]Quoted in Eberhard Arnold, *Love and Marriage in the Spirit* (Rifton, NY: Plough, 1965), 102.

[5]Friedrich E. F. von Gagern, *Der Mensch als Bild: Beiträge zur Anthropologie.* 2nd ed. (Frankfurt am Main: Verlag Josef Knecht, 1955), 32.

[6]Quoted in Hans Meier, *Solange das Licht Brennt* (Norfolk, CT: Hutterian Brethren, 1990), 17.

[7]*Der Mensch als Bild*, 33–34.

[8]Dietrich Bonhoeffer, *Ethics* (New York: Macmillan, 1975), 19.

[9]*Der Mensch als Bild*, 58.

[10]*Love and Marriage in the Spirit*, 152.

[11]J. Heinrich Arnold, *Discipleship* (Farmington, PA: Plough, 1994), 42.

[12]Eberhard Arnold, *Inner Land* (Rifton, NY: Plough, 1976), 55–56.

[13]Dietrich Bonhoeffer, *The Cost of Discipleship* (New York: Macmillan, 1958) 95–96.

[14]Cf. Peter Riedemann, *Confession of Faith* (1540), (Rifton, NY: Plough, 1974), 98.

[15]*Discipleship*, 160–161.

[16]Ernst Rolffs, ed., *Tertullian, der Vater des abendländischen Christentums: Ein Kämpfer für und gegen die römische Kirche* (Berlin: Hochweg, 1930), 31–32.

[17]Jean Vanier, *Man and Woman He Made Them* (New York: Paulist, 1994), 128.

[18]Friedrich von Gagern, *Man and Woman: An Introduction to the Mystery of Marriage* (Cork, Ireland: Mercier, 1957), 26–27.

[19]I explore this theme in greater depth in my book *A Little Child Shall Lead Them: Hopeful Parenting in a Confused World* (Farmington, PA: Plough, 1997).

[20]Johann Christoph and Christoph Friedrich Blumhardt, *Thoughts About Children* (Rifton, NY: Plough, 1980), 29.

[21]*Thoughts About Children*, 9.

[22]*Discipleship*, 169.

[23]*Discipleship*, 177–178.

[24]Dietrich Bonhoeffer, *The Martyred Christian: 160 Readings* (New York: Collier Macmillan, 1985), 170.

[25]Eberhard Arnold, *The Early Christians* (Rifton, NY: Plough, 1972), 18.

[26]*The Wall Street Journal*, Dec. 10, 1993.

[27]Numerous studies, including those conducted by Planned Parenthood, conclude that teens who have been through a typical sex education course have a fifty percent higher rate of sexual activity than those who have not. For more information on teenage sexual activity contact: Center for Parent/Youth Understanding, P.O. Box 414, Elizabethtown, PA 17022 Tel: (717) 361-8429

[28]"Church report accepts cohabiting couples." *The Tablet*, June 10, 1995.

[29]Thomas E. Schmidt, *Straight and Narrow? Compassion and Clarity in the Homosexuality Debate* (Downers Grove, IL: InterVarsity, 1995), 131–159.

[30]In *Straight and Narrow?* (pp. 153–159 in particular), Schmidt discusses various programs and organizations for men and women seeking a way out of the homosexual lifestyle. See For Further Reading for more about this book.

[31]Eberhard Arnold, *God's Revolution* (Farmington, PA: Plough, 1992), 151.

[32]Stanley Hauerwas, *Unleashing the Scripture: Freeing the Bible from Captivity to America* (Nashville: Abingdon, 1993), 131.

[33]Michael J. Gorman, *Abortion and the Early Church: Christian, Jewish, and Pagan Attitudes in the Greco-Roman World* (New York: Paulist, 1982), 47–62.

[34]*Ethics*, 164.

[35]*Inner Land*, 155.

[36]Frederica Mathewes-Green, "Perspective." *The Plough* 56 (Spring 1998), 33.

[37]If divorce and remarriage are never justified, then why does Jesus allow marital unfaithfulness as an exception? (Matt. 5:32,19:9) Without going into great detail, two things can be said. First, in Jesus' day a husband was required, by Jewish law, to divorce an adulterous wife (e.g. Matt. 1:19). Thus, in Matt. 5:32, Jesus is saying that a man who divorces his unfaithful wife (which the law required he do) is not responsible, by this action, for her adultery. In any other kind of divorce, however, he is the culpable one; the adulterer. This does not mean that divorce is ever justifiable or required. When we come later to Matt. 19:9, then, the exception of marital unfaithfulness should be read to apply to divorce only and not to remarriage.

[38]For a detailed account of how divorce affects children, see chapter 5 of Glenn T. Stanton's *Why Marriage Matters: Reasons to Believe in Marriage in Postmodern Society*. (Colorado Springs, CO: Pinon Press, 1997).

For Further Reading

Arnold, Eberhard. *God's Revolution*. Farmington, PA: Plough, 1983. Topically arranged excerpts from the author's talks and writings on community, marriage, the family, children, and the church.

Arnold, J. Christoph. *Endangered: Your Child in a Hostile World*. Farmington, PA: Plough, 2000. From ordinary educators and parents, real stories of empowerment and hopes against all odds.

Arnold, J. Christoph. *A Little Child Shall Lead Them: Hopeful Parenting in a Confused World*. Farmington, PA: Plough, 1997. Practical and down to earth advice on raising and educating children.

Arnold, J. Heinrich. *Discipleship*. Farmington, PA: Plough, 1994. Thoughts on following Christ in the daily grind, topically arranged. Includes sections on sex, love, marriage, parenting, and celibacy.

__________________. *Freedom From Sinful Thoughts*. Rifton, NY: Plough, 1997. Spiritual insights on the struggle to overcome personal sins and temptations.

Bloesch, Donald G. *Is the Bible Sexist?* Westchester, IL: Crossway, 1982. A sane and sober approach to the volatile issue of feminism in the church that is both sensitive to women's concerns *and* solidly grounded in the Bible.

Bonhoeffer, Dietrich. *Life Together*. New York: Harper and Brothers, 1954. A time-honored manifesto on one the most essential aspects of being: solitude, interaction, and community.

Chesterton, G.K. *Brave New Family*. San Francisco: Ignatius, 1990. Prophetic and insightful essays on love, sex, marriage, gender roles, children, and the institution of the family in western society.

Clapp, Rodney. *Families at the Crossroads*. Downers Grove, IL: InterVarsity, 1993. A thoughtful discussion on the role of the church in family life from a biblical perspective.

Cornes, Andrew. *Divorce and Remarriage*. Grand Rapids, MI: Eerdmans, 1993. The most thorough biblical and pastoral treatment of this difficult subject to date.

Fromm, Erich. *The Art of Loving*. New York: Harper Collins, 1989. Reflections on the definition and meaning of love.

Gagern, Friedrich E. F. von. *Difficulties in Married Life*. New York: Paulist, 1964. Thoughtful advice from an experienced Catholic psychiatrist.

__________________. *Man and Woman: An Introduction to the Mystery of Marriage*. Cork, Ireland: Mercier, 1957. Sex education with an emphasis on reverence as the key to a healthy sexuality.

Gorman, Michael J. *Abortion and the Early Church*. New York: Paulist, 1982. A readable and concise treatment on the early church's stand against abortion.

Harris, Joshua. *I Kissed Dating Goodbye*. Sisters, OR: Multnomah Books, 1997. This book shows the pitfalls of the conventional dating game and points young adults toward a lifestyle of purity, in which true friendships can blossom.

Hildebrand, Dietrich von. *Purity: The Mystery of Christian Sexuality*. Steubenville, OH: Franciscan University Press, 1989. A masterful work on the meaning of purity – and Christ's call to a pure life.

__________________. *Man and Woman: Love and the Meaning of Intimacy*. Manchester, NH: Sophia Institute, 1992. A lucid discussion of the nature of love and the mystery of sexuality.

Laney, J. Carl. *The Divorce Myth*. Minneapolis: Bethany House, 1981. A compassionate but uncompromising challenge to the institutions of divorce and remarriage, from a biblical perspective.

Mathewes-Green, Frederica. *Real Choices: Listening to Women; Looking for Alternatives to Abortion*. Ben Lomond, CA: Conciliar Press, 1997. A sensitive look at the real reasons why women choose abortion and how to help them find meaningful alternatives.

Neuer, Werner. *Man and Woman in Christian Perspective*. Wheaton, IL: Crossway, 1991. A biblical discussion of the similarities and differences between men and women.

Schmidt, Thomas E. *Straight and Narrow? Compassion and Clarity in the Homosexuality Debate*. Downers Grove, IL: InterVarsity, 1995. A frank but uncompromising scriptural treatment of homosexuality.

Stanton, Glenn T. *Why Marriage Matters: Reasons to Believe in Marriage in Postmodern Society*. Colorado Springs, CO: Pinon Press, 1997. This book is a highly readable presentation of up-to-date research on the dire consequences of marital breakdown in our society.

Vanier, Jean. *Community and Growth*. New York: Paulist, 1989. A bestselling collection of readings, topically arranged, calling for a radical turn from the disintegration and divisiveness of contemporary society to love, mutual support, and community.